GETTING READY

FOR THE

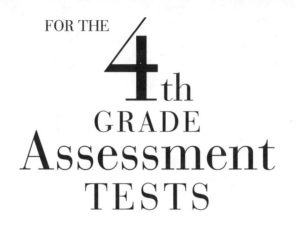

4th
GRADE
Assessment
TESTS

GETTING READY

FOR THE

4th

GRADE

Assessment

TESTS

Improve Your Child's
Math and English Skills

Erika Warecki

NEW YORK

Library of Congress Cataloging-in-Publication Data:
Warecki, Erika.
    Getting ready for the 4th grade assessment tests : improve your child's math and
English skills / Erika Warecki.—1st ed.
        p. cm.
ISBN 1-57685-416-7 (alk. paper)
  1. Educational tests and measurements—United States. 2. Fourth grade (Educa-
tion)—United States. 3. Education, Elementary—Parent participation—United
States. I. Title: Getting ready for the fourth grade assessment tests. II. Title.
    LB3060.22 .W27 2002
    372.126'2—dc21
                                                                    2002001845

Printed in the United States of America

9 8 7 6 5 4 3 2 1

First Edition

ISBN 1-57685-416-7

For more information or to place an order, contact LearningExpress at:
    900 Broadway
    Suite 604
    New York, NY 10003

Or visit us at:
    www.learnatest.com

CONTENTS

INTRODUCTION

Let's face it—there is no escaping them. Standardized tests are here to stay, and there are more of them now than when we were kids. Not only that, the tests are a lot harder! As parents, you may feel confused about how you can best help your child prepare and succeed on the fourth grade assessment tests. This book will help you in your quest because its purpose is to outline what your child is expected to know and how that knowledge will be tested.

Think of it this way. Taking a standardized test is like taking a driver's test. Before you take the test, you study the rules of the road, get a learner's permit, practice, practice, practice, and then you take your road test. The fourth grade tests are not any different, in theory that is. The rules of the road are not stop signs or traffic lights, but instead they are called *state standards*. Administrators and teachers use them to prepare their lessons, and by doing so they make sure that your child gets the best education possible. But, here is where the metaphor starts to fall apart. Unlike a fledgling driver who needs a permit to practice, your child is automatically considered a student. As a parent, you know that sometimes the pressure of the school day, the homework, and the anxiety of taking a standardized test can be daunting for any fourth grader. Here is where you come in. Involved parents working together with experienced teachers are the best coaches. As you practice the exercises in this book with your child, you are taking one of your first steps toward preparation. But, first, you should know the timeframe.

Since each state has its own standards, each state also sets its own testing schedule. Some tests are administered during the winter months, others during the spring. Some tests are given over a period of a few days, especially English Language Arts, while other subjects—like math—are given in one day. Exact dates change from year to year, and in that case you should contact your child's school administrators, your child's teacher, or visit your state's educational website, but a list of approximate dates is provided for you below.

ALABAMA

Name of test:	SAT 9
Subjects covered:	Reading, Writing, Math, Science, Social Science
Month given:	April

ARIZONA

Name of test:	SAT 9
Subjects covered:	Reading, Writing, Math
Month given:	March

ARKANSAS

Name of test:	SAT 9
Subjects covered:	Reading, Writing, Math
Month given:	April

CALIFORNIA

Name of test:	SAT 9 and Standardized Testing and Reporting (STAR)
Subjects covered:	Reading, Writing, Math
Month given:	March

COLORADO

Name of test:	Colorado Student Assessment Program (CSAP)
Subjects covered:	Reading, Writing
Month given:	March/April

CONNECTICUT

Name of test:	Connecticut Mastery Test (CMT)
Subjects covered:	Reading, Writing, Math
Month given:	September/October

DELAWARE

Name of test:	Delaware Student Testing Program (DSTP)
Subjects covered:	Science, Social Science
Month given:	N/A

FLORIDA

Name of test:	Florida Comprehensive Assessment Test (FCAT)
Subjects covered:	Reading, Math
Month given:	January/March

IDAHO

Name of test: Iowa Test of Basic Skills
Subjects covered: Reading, Writing, Math
Month given: October/November

ILLINOIS

Name of test: Illinois Standards Achievement Test (ISAT)
Subjects covered: Science, Social Science
Month given: April

IOWA

Name of test: Iowa Test of Basic Skills (ITBS)
Subjects covered: Reading, Writing, Math
Month given: N/A

KANSAS

Name of test: Criterion Based State Assessment
Subjects covered: Math, Science
Month given: February/March

KENTUCKY

Name of test: Commonwealth Accountability Testing System (CATS)
Subjects covered: Reading, Writing, Math
Month given: April/May

LOUISIANA

Name of test: Iowa Tests of Educational Development (ITED)
Subjects covered: Reading, Writing, Math
Month given: March

MAINE

Name of test: Maine Educational Assessment (MEA)
Subjects covered: Reading, Writing, Math, Science, Social Science, Arts
Month given: March/November/December

MASSACHUSETTS

Name of test: Massachusetts Comprehensive Assessment System
Subjects covered: Reading, Writing, Math
Month given: April/May

MISSISSIPPI

Name of test: Terra Nova
Subjects covered: Reading, Writing, Math
Month given: May

MISSOURI

Name of test: Missouri Assessment Program (MAP)
Subjects covered: Math, Reading
Month given: April/May

MONTANA

Name of test: Iowa Test of Basic Skills
Subjects covered: Reading, Writing, Math, Science, Social Science
Month given: March

NORTH CAROLINA

Name of test: North Carolina Testing Program
Subjects covered: Reading, Writing, Math
Month given: last month of school

NORTH DAKOTA

Name of test: Terra Nova
Subjects covered: Reading, Writing, Math, Science, Social Science
Month given: March

NEVADA

Name of test: Terra Nova
Subjects covered: Reading, Writing, Math, Science, Social Science
Month given: October

NEW JERSEY

Name of test: Elementary School Proficiency Assessment (ESPA)
Subjects covered: Reading, Math
Month given: May

NEW MEXICO

Name of test: Mew Mexico Achievement Assessment
Subjects covered: Reading, Writing, Math
Month given: March

NEW YORK

Name of test: Fourth Grade Assessment
Subjects covered: Reading, Math
Month given: January/May

OHIO

Name of test: Ohio Proficiency Test
Subjects covered: Reading, Writing, Math, Citizenship, Science
Month given: March

RHODE ISLAND

Name of test: National Academy of Educational Progress (NAEP)
Subjects covered: Reading, Writing, Math
Month given: February/March

SOUTH CAROLINA
Name of test:	Palmetto Achievement Challenge Test (PACT)
Subjects covered:	Reading, Writing, Math
Month given:	April/May

SOUTH DAKOTA
Name of test:	SAT 9
Subjects covered:	Reading, Writing, Math, Science, Social Science
Month given:	March/April

TENNESSEE
Name of test:	Terra Nova
Subjects covered:	Reading, Writing, Math, Science, Social Science
Month given:	March/April

TEXAS
Name of test:	Texas Assessment of Academic Skills (TAAS)
Subjects covered:	Reading, Writing, Math
Month given:	May

VERMONT
Name of test:	Vermont Comprehensive Assessment System (VCAS)
Subjects covered:	Reading, Writing, Math
Month given:	March

VIRGINIA
Name of test:	SAT 9
Subjects covered:	Reading, Writing, Math
Month given:	April or May (school's choice)

WASHINGTON
Name of test:	Washington Assessment of Student Learning
Subjects covered:	Reading, Writing, Math
Month given:	April/May

WASHINGTON, DC
Name of test:	SAT 9
Subjects covered:	Reading, Writing, Math
Month given:	April

WEST VIRGINIA
Name of test:	SAT 9
Subjects covered:	Reading, Writing, Math, Science, Social Science
Month given:	April

Name of test: Wisconsin Knowledge and Concepts Examination (WKCE)

Subjects covered: Reading, Writing, Math

Month given: February/March

Name of test: Wyoming Comprehensive Assessment System (Terra Nova and Content Standards)

Subjects covered: Reading, Writing, Math

Month given: March

How to Use This Book

IN THIS BOOK, you will find the standards for English Language Arts and Math spelled out very clearly. Then you will be given sample exercises in both subjects. Set aside some special time every day to work with your child on these sections. Not only is this beneficial to the parent/child relationship, but it will build confidence, self-esteem, and a sense of preparedness in your child that many other children will not have.

As you work through each reading comprehension question, essay, or math problem, you may find that there are some questions you are unsure about. In that case, an answer key and an answer explanation guide has been provided that walks you through each math problem, explains each reading comprehension question, and gives you practical advice for responding to essays. There are some very general rubrics provided as well. If you have never heard the term *rubric*, don't let that scare you. It is a somewhat educational word that essentially means scoring guide. With some practice and some directions, you will be given the tools you need to find out just exactly how states determine essay grades.

Math

TO GUIDE YOUR child to mastery in mathematics, all states have written standards that students must reach. The following sections contain the kind of math your child will need to know and the kind of math that is tested by most states.

Mathematical Reasoning
Number and Numeration
Operations
Modeling/Multiple Representation
Measurement
Uncertainty
Patterns/Functions

MATHEMATICAL REASONING

Students must know how to use mathematical reasoning to analyze mathematical situations, gather evidence, make conjectures, and construct an argument.

Students must be able to draw conclusions and explain their thinking using models, facts, and relationships. They must analyze mathematical situations and justify their answers, as well as use logical reasoning to reach simple conclusions.

NUMBER AND NUMERATION

Students must be able to use number sense to develop an understanding of the many uses of numbers in the real world. They must be able to use numbers to communicate mathematically and in the development of mathematical ideas.

They must use whole numbers, fractions, decimals, place value, percent, and number order.

OPERATIONS

Students must use mathematical operations and the relationships among them to understand mathematics.

They must add, subtract, multiply, and divide whole numbers, as well as know single digit addition, subtraction, multiplication and division facts. They must also know the commutative and associative properties.

MODELING/MULTIPLE REPRESENTATION

Students must be able to provide a means of presenting, interpreting, communicating, and connecting mathematical information using mathematical modeling/multiple representation.

They must construct tables, charts, and graphs to display data. They must also use variables such as height and weight to predict changes over time.

MEASUREMENT

Students must be able to use both English measure and metric to describe and compare objects and data. They must understand area, length, capacity, weight, volume, time, temperature, and angle. They must also be able to estimate and find measures such as length, perimeter, area, and volume. Not only that, but they must also collect and display data, as well as use graphs, tables, and charts to interpret data.

UNCERTAINTY

Uncertainty is probability and statistics. Students must realize things are not always exact in the real world. Students should be able to estimate and compare estimates to actual results, recognize when only an estimate is required, predict possibilities, make predictions using random samples, and determine probabilities of simple events.

Students must recognize, describe, create, and extend a wide variety of patterns. They also must interpret graphs and explore and develop relationships among two-and three-dimensional geometric shapes.

To measure knowledge and skills, your child will have to take a standardized test. All standardized math tests are presented as multiple-choice and open-ended questions. Everyone knows what a multiple-choice question is, but not everyone knows the easiest way to go about choosing the correct answer. Believe it or not, it's not always about solving the problem. Of course, that's part of it. But, those skilled in test-taking will tell you there is more to the science of multiple-choice than just mathematical skill. Hints and advice are offered along the way in this book.

English/Language Arts

TO GUIDE YOUR child to mastery in English/Language Arts, all states have written standards that students must reach. While wording may vary from state to state, they are all similar in design. Your child will be tested on three main standards:

▶ **Literary Response and Expression**: Your child will not only read, but listen to passages, and must be able to relate these passages to his or her own life. Not only that, but your child must be able to write down his or her own ideas, using correct English, including grammar, spelling, usage, and punctuation.

▶ **Critical Analysis and Evaluation**: Your child must be able to analyze ideas presented by others. He or she also must be able to convey individual opinions on ideas and information.

▶ **Information and Understanding**: Your child will have to collect data, facts and ideas, find relationships, concepts, and make generalizations. He or she also has to acquire information and be able to interpret it.

English/Language Arts assessment tests always have reading passages with multiple-choice questions. In many states, your child will also have to listen to a passage, take notes on it, and then use those notes to answer questions. Often, the notes taken during the listening section are the only reference students have when responding to questions. Since, students cannot look at the passage again, these note taking skills are very, very important. Your child also may have to read related passages and respond to short and long response questions. Your fourth grader has to know some pretty sophisticated skills to analyze and explain how one reading relates and compares to other readings. Some questions require students to interpret and draw conclusions from an article, illustration, or graph. In addition, at some point on the English/Language Arts assessment tests, your child will have to write a short composition. Students must write clear, complete responses.

The kind of literary skills that are tested on most English/Language Arts assessment tests are as follows:

- ▶ identify the main idea of a passage
- ▶ use evidence from stories to identify characters
- ▶ pick out the supporting details
- ▶ understand story events
- ▶ use strategies to construct meaning
- ▶ locate information to solve a problem
- ▶ use vocabulary strategies
- ▶ use critical analysis to identify point of view
- ▶ make inferences regarding character motivation
- ▶ use critical analysis to evaluate ideas based on prior knowledge/personal experience
- ▶ recognize how language is used to persuade
- ▶ draw conclusions about characters and events

Teaching to the Test

YOU MAY HEAR some parents complain that schools aren't teaching children as effectively as they used to. They say that teachers are only *teaching to* the tests. While it does seem that teachers spend a lot of time preparing for assessment tests, it is also true that while they do this, they are teaching important skills that students will use later on in life. Very often though, this is questioned.

At some point, most every student asks, "Why do we have to learn this?" Fast forward to the future. Your child, now an adult, enters the voting booth. Had he not learned how to compare and contrast fictional characters from short stories and books in Mr. Sherman's class, would he be able to skillfully assess the correct candidate for the job? Would she be able to analyze all of the political ideas presented before a very important presidential election if she not read and analyzed nonfiction passages and books in class? Would he be able to choose the best finance director knowledgeably had he not learned to interpret the data from the graphs and charts in his class exercises? If your schools are living up to the state standards outlined above, they are teaching everything a child needs to know to succeed.

Basic Hints for Success
on Any Fourth Grade Assessment Test

▶ **Be consistent:** Don't change your child's bedtime routine or morning routine on the day of the test. This could be too disruptive and cause undue stress. Let bedtimes, wake-up times, and meals be ordinary.

▶ **Be comfortable:** Let your child wear comfortable clothes, and dress in layers. If it is too hot in the room, he or she can take a sweatshirt off and still have a comfortable tee-shirt on underneath. Comfortable shoes are a good idea too.

▶ **Be careful:** Tell your child to listen carefully to all instructions and pay close attention when the teacher is explaining directions and schedules.

▶ **Be prepared:** Have your child bring extra pencils that are already sharpened. If a pencil point breaks in the middle of taking the test, he or she won't have to waste time sharpening it.

▶ **Be neat:** Fill in the bubbles to the multiple choice questions neatly and completely. This is one time to tell your little artist to "stay within the lines."

▶ **Be time conscious:** If your child is having trouble with one question, make sure he or she knows not to take too much time trying to figure it out. It is best, in that case, to eliminate the obvious wrong answers and make the best possible guess. If there is extra time at the end of the test, he or she can go back and review an answer.

More Good Ideas

▶ Limit your child's television watching and video game usage.

▶ Ask your child to tell you about what he or she is reading.

▶ Make sure your child completes all of his or her homework and class work.

▶ Have discussions with your child about his studies.

▶ Read aloud with your child, and encourage him or her to keep a journal. Before bedtime, you can spend time together writing in your journals. (They can be real, like a diary, or fictional.)

Ruler   Counters   Pattern Blocks

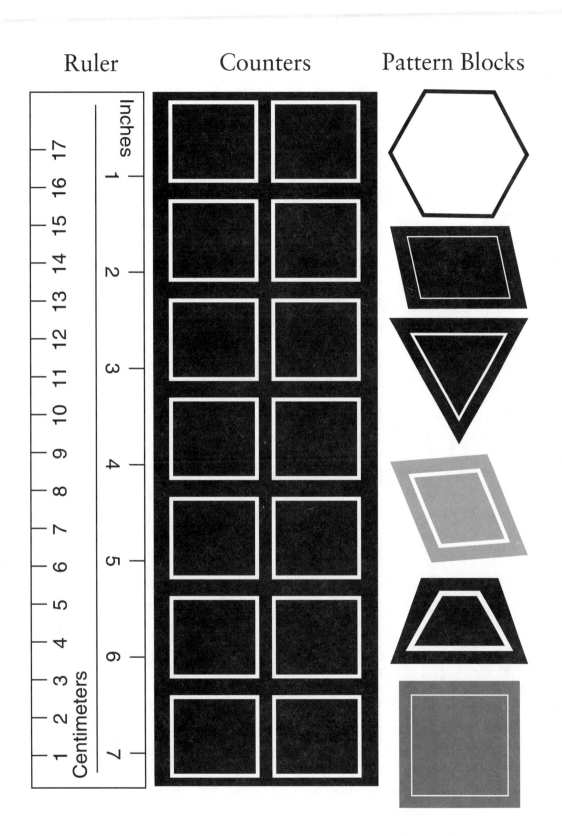

GETTING READY

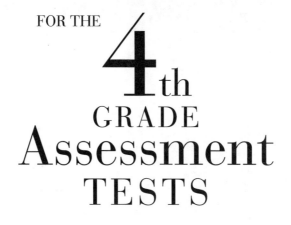

FOR THE
4th
GRADE
Assessment
TESTS

CHAPTER

Math Practice

On **most** fourth grade assessment tests, there aren't many straightforward addition or subtraction questions, where your child is asked to add or subtract whole numbers. Usually he or she is asked to add or subtract decimals or fractions, to estimate numbers, and *then* to add or subtract them. These are called *questions of combined operations*; for example: If Bill has 10 dollars and gets another 8, but then spends 9, how much does he have left? In this question, it is up to your child to figure out which operations to perform, and in which order. It does not say, "First add 10 and 8, and then minus 9 from your answer." Your child must figure out from the wording of a problem what is expected. For example, "how much does he have left?" indicates that the second part of the problem is subtraction.

It is always a good idea to review the basics, mainly for the practice, but also because they will be asked in various ways. The following sections build addition and subtraction skills and then work on combined operations skills. First, we will go over addition and subtraction, followed by multiplication, division, and combined operations. Next, there will be questions on estimating, decimals, fractions, patterns, and time. The last sections will cover various questions in geometry and place value.

Two other things your child must know are the commutative and associative properties. The commutative property is $a + b = b + a$, or $a \times b = b \times a$. The associative property is $(a + b) + c = a + (b + c)$ or $(a \times b) \times c = a \times (b \times c)$.

Addition

WHEN DOING ADDITION problems, look for the common phrases used, such as *how many in all, how many altogether* or *find the sum*. These all refer to adding the given numbers together. It is always important when doing addition problems to watch out for careless mistakes.

1. What is $(3 + 5) + 6$?
    a. $7 + 6 = 13$
    b. $8 + 6 = 14$
    c. $9 + 6 = 15$
    d. none of the above

2. Solve $(11 + 3) + 7$.
    a. 20
    b. 21
    c. 22
    d. 23

3. Joyce's family took a long car trip. They traveled 651 miles the first day, 491 the second day, and 537 miles the third day. How many miles did they travel altogether?
    a. 1,142
    b. 1,689
    c. 1,679
    d. 1,028

4. Jaclyn went food shopping and spent $57 the first week, $36 the second, $43 the third, and $35 the fourth. How much did she spend altogether?
    a. $161
    b. $170
    c. $171
    d. $172

5. Calculate the sum of 4,321 and 6,746, added to 938.
    a. 12,005
    b. 12,004
    c. 11,067
    d. 10,129

6. Solve $(8,964 + 2,876) + 1,123$.
    a. 12,963
    b. 11,963
    c. 12,964
    d. 11,840

7. Louisa and her family picked cherries one afternoon. In one bucket, Louisa counted 374 cherries, and in another bucket she counted 287 cherries. How many cherries were there in the 2 buckets?
   a. 662
   b. 661
   c. 652
   d. 651

8. Two basketball teams were having a competition to see who could collect the most canned food. One team collected 470 cans and the other team collected 590 cans. How many cans were there altogether?
   a. 920
   b. 960
   c. 1,060
   d. 1,070

9. $279 + 68 =$
   a. 211
   b. 237
   c. 337
   d. 347

10. The Paulson family drove 1,102 miles from Los Angeles to Cheyenne, Wyoming. From Cheyenne they drove 1,158 miles to Portland, Oregon. From Portland they drove 967 miles back to Los Angeles. What was the total distance of the Paulson's trip?
    a. 11,930 miles
    b. 3,227 miles
    c. 2,260 miles
    d. 2,117 miles

Subtraction

WHEN DOING SUBTRACTION problems, look for clue phrases such as *how many were left*. Be careful when regrouping. Use plenty of scrap paper if you need to.

11. Brian had 738 baseball cards. He gave away 193 of them. How many does he have left?
    a. 544
    b. 545
    c. 595
    d. 445

12. Mrs. Heinz brought in one cupcake each for the 24 children in her class. If 5 children were absent that day, how many cupcakes were eaten?
    a. 17
    b. 18
    c. 19
    d. 20

13. Calculate 4,321 − 1,234.
    a. 1,234
    b. 123
    c. 3,012
    d. 3,087

14. Subtract 9,381 from 10,702.
    a. 19,083
    b. 20,083
    c. 1,331
    d. 1,321

15. There were 832 students at North Lake Elementary School. When 63 students moved away, how many were left?
    a. 769
    b. 779
    c. 879
    d. 895

16. On Betty's favorite video game, the highest score ever made is 9,689. The highest score Betty has made is 6,752. What is the difference between Betty's score and the highest score?
    a. 2,927
    b. 2,937
    c. 3,927
    d. 3,937

17.   805
    −382
    a. 423
    b. 523
    c. 583
    d. 1,187

Multiplication

WHEN DOING MULTIPLICATION problems, make sure you do what is in the parentheses first. Multiplication is just a fast way of adding the same number a certain amount of times, so you may still see similar phrases like *how many in all*. This is because, for example, 3×4 is really the same thing as $3 + 3 + 3 + 3$.

18. Brittany is having a party with 15 of her friends. She wants to have 2 party favors and 5 lollipops for each friend. How many party favors and lollipops must she buy?
    a. 75 party favors and 75 lollipops
    b. 75 party favors and 30 lollipops
    c. 30 party favors and 75 lollipops
    d. 30 party favors and 30 lollipops

19. What is $(4 \times 4) + (3 \times 3)$ equal to?
    a. 25
    b. 16
    c. 9
    d. 7

20. Calculate $(7 \times 8) - 14$.
    a. 50
    b. 42
    c. 56
    d. 1

21. $(6 \times 8) - (3 \times 4) =$
    a. 52
    b. 42
    c. 7
    d. 36

22. Jane is putting a fence around her square garden. She needs 5 yards of fencing for each side of the garden. How many yards of fencing must she purchase?
    a. $5 + 4 = 9$ yards
    b. $5 \times 4 = 20$ yards
    c. $5 \times 5 = 25$ yards
    d. none of the above

23. Calculate $(7 \times 4) + 43$.
    a. 1,204
    b. 71
    c. 54
    d. 72

24. Farmer Sam has 34 chickens and each chicken lays 27 eggs per day. How many eggs do they lay in one full week?
    a. 918
    b. 6,426
    c. 4,590
    d. 6,664

25. Vanessa has a book that is 98 pages long. If it takes her 3 minutes to read 1 page, how long will it take her to read the entire book?
    a. 32 minutes
    b. 98 minutes
    c. 294 minutes
    d. 394 minutes

26. The Richards farm has 17 cows and each cow produces 38 quarts of milk per day. How many quarts of milk are produced each day?
    a. 546 quarts
    b. 380 quarts
    c. 55 quarts
    d. 646 quarts

27. At Lewin's Farms, workers pick 234 baskets of apples each day. Each basket holds 51 apples. How many apples are picked each day?
    a. 821
    b. 10,934
    c. 11,934
    d. 285

28. Alija has harvested watermelons. He has 264 rows of watermelons, and there are 437 watermelons in each row. How many watermelons does Alija grow?
    a. 115,368
    b. 3,696
    c. 701
    d. 116,368

29. Jamie has 24 chocolate chip cookies. Each cookie has 7 chips in it. How many chocolate chips are there in all?
    a. 24
    b. 168
    c. 31
    d. 158

30. For Halloween, Annie made 54 goodie bags. Each bag has 8 pieces of candy in it. How many pieces of candy are there in all?
    a. 480
    b. 62
    c. 432
    d. 424

31.   34
    $\times 21$

    a. 614
    b. 646
    c. 714
    d. 1,020

32.   28
    $\times 13$

    a. 112
    b. 354
    c. 364
    d. 464

33. Ms. Friedman had 15 peach trees. On each tree, there were 23 peaches. How many peaches were there?
    a. 38
    b. 245
    c. 335
    d. 345

34.   539
    $\times 62$

    a. 33,448
    b. 33,418
    c. 33,318
    d. 32,418

35. $3 \times 285 =$
    a. 655
    b. 845
    c. 855
    d. 1,255

36. Mr. Bosco's car uses one gallon of gas to drive 34 miles. Last month the car used 27 gallons of gas. How many miles did Mr. Bosco drive last month?
    a. 306
    b. 918
    c. 1,038
    d. 1,378

37. The Fun-Rail train has 16 cars. Each car can hold 24 passengers. How many people can ride on the Fun-Rail train at one time?
    a. 40
    b. 102
    c. 384
    d. 544

38. Anna ordered 17 boxes of the beads shown below.

    675
    Beads

    How many beads did she order in all?
    a. 4,970
    b. 5,390
    c. 11,045
    d. 11,475

Division

39. Calculate 64 ÷ 4.
    a. 21
    b. 14
    c. 18
    d. 16

40. If Michael had a pizza pie cut into 8 slices and he invited Kevin to share with him, how many slices would each boy get?
    a. 1
    b. 2
    c. 4
    d. 8

41. 63 ÷ 7 =
    a. 7
    b. 8
    c. 8 with a remainder of 6
    d. 9

42. $82 \div 9 =$
   a. 9
   b. 9 with a remainder of 1
   c. 9 with a remainder of 2
   d. 10

43. $(16 \div 4) + 3 =$
   a. 19
   b. 7
   c. 15
   d. 23

44. $(42 \div 6) - 5 =$
   a. 2
   b. 3
   c. 42
   d. 37

45. $(27 \div 3) + 4 =$
   a. 7
   b. 9
   c. 11
   d. 13

46. Paula's Music Store has 378 CDs. The store sells 7 CDs per day. How many days will it take to sell all of the CDs?
   a. 54 days
   b. 2,646 days
   c. 378 days
   d. 7 days

47. Harper's Toy Factory puts 6 dolls in each box. The factory made 2,442 dolls. How many boxes will they need?
   a. 14,652
   b. 244
   c. 47
   d. 407

48. Cicerelli's Book Store puts 60 books on each shelf. How many shelves will they need for 2,520 books?
   a. 42
   b. 60
   c. 420
   d. 100

49. What is $874 \div 8$?
   a. 108
   b. 109 with a remainder of 1
   c. 109 with a remainder of 2
   d. 109

50. The Leary Farm has 720 chickens. The chickens are kept in 20 coops. How many chickens are in each coop?
   a. 10
   b. 72
   c. 30
   d. 36

51. Judy had 225 pieces of candy and 25 goodie bags. If she puts an equal amount of candy in each bag, how many pieces does each bag get?
   a. 8
   b. 9
   c. 10
   d. 11

52. $\frac{74}{8} =$
   a. 7
   b. 8 with a remainder of 2
   c. 9
   d. 9 with a remainder of 2

53. Mr. Schwab's orchard has 12 rows of trees. Each row has the same number of trees. If there are 72 trees altogether, how many trees are in each row?
   a. 8
   b. 7
   c. 6
   d. 5

54. At a Fourth of July party, there were 49 cookies to decorate and 7 people to decorate them. If each person decorated the same number, how many cookies did each person decorate?
   a. 5
   b. 7
   c. 8
   d. 9

55. $\frac{70}{9} =$
   a. 5
   b. 6 with a remainder of 6
   c. 7
   d. 7 with a remainder of 7

56. $7\overline{)167} =$
   a. 21 with a remainder of 2
   b. 22 with a remainder of 15
   c. 23 with a remainder of 6
   d. 24

57. $69 \div 4 =$
   a. 12
   b. 17
   c. 12 with a remainder of 3
   d. 17 with a remainder of 1

58. Akiko used 588 beads to make 6 bracelets. Each bracelet has the same number of beads. How many beads does each bracelet have?
   a. 83
   b. 89
   c. 98
   d. 104

59. Miss Duval ordered 420 bath towels to sell in her store. The towels were packed in 12 boxes when they arrived. If each box had the same number of towels, how many towels were in each box?
   a. 33
   b. 35
   c. 41
   d. 350

Combined Operations

60. In the pond there were 364 trout and 241 bass. A fishing expedition caught 123 fish. How many fish are left in the pond?
   a. 605
   b. 482
   c. 241
   d. 118

61. Emily has $16. She spends $4 on a movie ticket, $2 on a soda and $3 on a bag of popcorn. How much does she have left?
   a. 5
   b. 6
   c. 7
   d. 8

62. Mrs. Weeks gave her twins Katie and Allie 4 cookies each. Mrs. Marciano gave her triplets Lauren, Jenna, and Steven 6 cookies each. How many cookies were given out altogether?
    a. 10
    b. 13
    c. 14
    d. 26

63. Laura is building a cabinet. She has 23 nails in her toolbox and she finds 17 lying around her workshop. If she needs 60 nails altogether, how many more does she need to buy?
    a. 20
    b. 17
    c. 23
    d. 19

64. Calculate the product of 93 and 84, then add to 171.
    a. 7,983
    b. 7,812
    c. 177
    d. 348

65. Richard had 492 cards. He sold 233 of them. A week later he bought 42 new ones. How many does he have now?
    a. 302
    b. 259
    c. 233
    d. 301

66. Fran has $437 in her checking account. If she writes one check for $42 and then writes another check for $59, how much money does he have left?
    a. $101
    b. $336
    c. $335
    d. $538

67. Ben had several old books and magazines that he wanted to sell. He had 26 books and 33 magazines. After his friend Pat bought some books and magazines there were 21 books and 23 magazines left. How many books did Pat buy?
    a. 5
    b. 7
    c. 10
    d. 15

68. Graham is painting his house. It took 7 gallons of paint for the first half. Graham has used 2 gallons so far on the second half. Which expression could be used to find how many gallons he needs to finish painting his house?
    a. $7 - 2$
    b. $7 + 2$
    c. 7×2
    d. $2 - 7$

69. Mrs. Gundlach needs 135 bricks to finish a wall in her backyard. If bricks are only sold in groups of 25, how many bricks will she have to buy?
    a. 135
    b. 150
    c. 160
    d. 175

70. Aaron has 132 stickers. He wants to give each of his six cousins the same number of stickers. If Aaron wants to keep 42 stickers, how many stickers should he give each cousin?
    a. 7
    b. 15
    c. 22
    d. 29

71. Dulce had 872 baseball cards. She sold 207 to Shu and gave 18 cards to her little brother. How many baseball cards did Dulce have left?
    a. 1,090
    b. 683
    c. 665
    d. 647

Estimating

72. Rosa has $12.53 in her wallet. What is that amount rounded to the nearest dollar?
    a. $10
    b. $12
    c. $12.50
    d. $13

73. A block wall that has 51,471 blocks will be built along a new highway. What is the number of blocks rounded to the nearest thousand?
    a. 50,000
    b. 51,000
    c. 51,500
    d. 52,000

74. During the winter, Kent went sledding for 4 days straight. Each day, he went down his hill about 37 times. Which is the best estimate of the total number of times he went down the hill?
    a. less than 75
    b. between 75 and 125
    c. between 125 and 175
    d. more than 175

75. There are many animals on Oliver's farm. There are 23 pigs, 49 chickens, and 68 ducks. Which is the best estimate of the total number of the animals?
    a. less than 60
    b. between 60 and 120
    c. between 120 and 180
    d. more than 180

76. About 347 people come into Gloria's Bakery every day. Estimate the number of people who come into the store in 1 week if the store is open every day of the week?
    a. 350
    b. 1,050
    c. 2,450
    d. 4,900

77. The car Fritz wants to buy costs $9,460. He sold his old car for $4,950. Which is the best estimate of how much more money Fritz needs to buy the car he wants?
    a. less than $4,200
    b. between $4,200 and $4,700
    c. between $4,700 and $5,200
    d. more than $5,200

78. What is the estimated answer for 43 + 31? (Round to the nearest whole number.)
    a. 70
    b. 84
    c. 80
    d. 85

79. What is the estimated answer for 498 + 211? (Round to the nearest hundred.)
    a. 500 + 200 = 700
    b. 400 + 200 = 600
    c. 500 + 300 = 800
    d. none of the above

80. What is the estimated answer for 328 + 451? (Round to the nearest hundred.)
    a. 300 + 500 = 800
    b. 300 + 400 = 700
    c. 400 + 500 = 900
    d. 300 + 450 = 750

81. What is the estimated answer for 2,904 + 3,210? (Round to the nearest thousand.)
    a. 2,000 + 3,000 = 5,000
    b. 3,000 + 4,000 = 7,000
    c. 2,000 + 2,000 = 4,000
    d. 3,000 + 3,000 = 6,000

Decimals

82. At the grocery store, an 8-ounce box of crackers costs $6.49 and a 4-ounce box of crackers costs $3.29. If Rachel purchases two of the smaller boxes and one of the larger boxes, what is the total cost?
    a. $13.07
    b. $16.27
    c. $12.98
    d. $9.87

83. Stacy practiced her flute for 2.5 hours on Monday, 1.25 hours on Tuesday, and 1.35 hours on Wednesday. How many hours did she practice altogether?
    a. 4.75 hours
    b. 5.1 hours
    c. 3.85 hours
    d. 5 hours

84. Nicky bought a book at The Collins Book Store. It cost $8.97. He gave the cashier a $20 bill. How much change will he get back?
    a. $11.03
    b. $12.03
    c. $12
    d. $11.97

85. Susannah went on a car trip to visit her family. She bought gas 4 times during the trip. She got 9.1 gallons, 8.7 gallons, 7.3 gallons, and 6.4 gallons of gas. How much gas did she purchase in all?
    a. 30.5 gallons
    b. 31.5 gallons
    c. 315 gallons
    d. 31.4 gallons

86. Paula is watering all the plants in her greenhouse. On the first day she used 3.2 gallons of water, on the second day she used 4.5 gallons and on the third day she used 10 gallons. How many gallons did she use in all?
    a. 14.4 gallons
    b. 8.7 gallons
    c. 17.7 gallons
    d. 16.7 gallons

87. What is 4.3×5.2 ?
    a. 20.6
    b. 9.5
    c. 22.36
    d. 21.36

88. Mrs. Post had 7.4 yards of cloth. She used 3.9 yards to make a dress. How many yards did she have left?
    a. 4.3
    b. 4.5
    c. 3.9
    d. 3.5

89. Tony has 17.34 feet of rope. He uses 9.18 feet. How much does he have left?
    a. 7.16 feet
    b. 9.18 feet
    c. 8.16 feet
    d. 9.16 feet

90. What is the product of 1.8 and 7.6?
    a. 136.8
    b. 13.68
    c. 7.48
    d. 1.368

91. What is the sum of 88.23, 91.05, and 75.46?
    a. 254.74
    b. 179.28
    c. 166.51
    d. 254.36

Fractions

92. Mary needs $1\frac{1}{5}$ yards of cloth to make a shirt. She has $3\frac{2}{5}$ yards. How many yards will be left over after Mary makes her shirt?

    a. $2\frac{1}{2}$ yards

    b. $2\frac{1}{5}$ yards

    c. $1\frac{4}{5}$ yards

    d. $2\frac{2}{5}$ yards

93. Solve: $\frac{1}{7} + \frac{3}{7} =$

    a. $\frac{1}{7}$

    b. $\frac{3}{7}$

    c. $\frac{4}{7}$

    d. $\frac{4}{14}$

94. What is $\frac{3}{10} + \frac{6}{10}$?

    a. $\frac{9}{20}$

    b. $\frac{9}{10}$

    c. $\frac{4}{5}$

    d. $3\frac{6}{10}$

95. Freddy has $6\frac{3}{4}$ yards of fence. He uses $4\frac{1}{4}$ yards. How many yards does he have left?

    a. $3\frac{1}{2}$

    b. $3\frac{1}{4}$

    c. $2\frac{1}{4}$

    d. $2\frac{1}{2}$

96. John has $3\frac{1}{2}$ cookies. Evelyn has $4\frac{1}{2}$ cookies. How many cookies do they have in all?

    a. 7

    b. $7\frac{1}{2}$

    c. 8

    d. $8\frac{1}{2}$

97. What fraction of the oval is shaded?

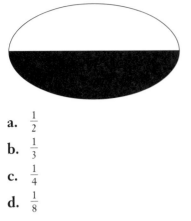

    a. $\frac{1}{2}$

    b. $\frac{1}{3}$

    c. $\frac{1}{4}$

    d. $\frac{1}{8}$

98. Which fraction matches the shaded part of the figure below?

    a. $\frac{1}{8}$

    b. $\frac{7}{8}$

    c. $\frac{7}{15}$

    d. $\frac{8}{15}$

99. Lamar made a pie for dinner. After dinner $\frac{1}{2}$ of the pie was left. Which of the pies below could be Lamar's?

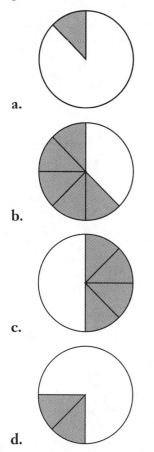

a.

b.

c.

d.

100. Which of the pictures below does NOT show $\frac{3}{4}$?

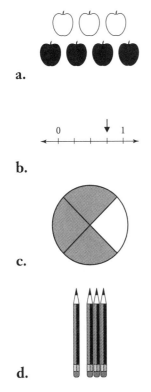

a.

b.

c.

d.

101. What fraction of the stickers shown below are hearts?

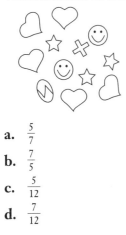

a. $\frac{5}{7}$

b. $\frac{7}{5}$

c. $\frac{5}{12}$

d. $\frac{7}{12}$

Patterns

102. If you continue the pattern, which number comes next?

    3, 6, 9, 12, ____

    a. 3
    b. 15
    c. 16
    d. 9

103. Barbara caught a cold and has to take her medicine at 1 o'clock, 3 o'clock, and 5 o'clock. If she continues this pattern, when is the next time she has to take her medicine?
    a. 1 o'clock
    b. 6 o'clock
    c. 7 o'clock
    d. 8 o'clock

104. Study the pattern below.

    ⫿⫿▭ ○ △⫿⫿▭ ○ △⫿⫿▭ ○ △⫿

    What is the next shape in the pattern?

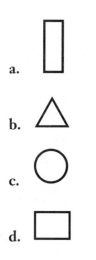

    a.

    b. △

    c. ○

    d. ▭

105. Study this number pattern.

7, 10, 13, 16, ___, 22, 25

What is the missing number?
a. 17
b. 18
c. 19
d. 20

106. Helen made a chart showing the number of minutes it took her to plant flowers.

Helen's Gardening

Number of Flowers	5	10	15
Number of Minutes	20	40	60

Based on the number pattern shown in the chart, how many minutes should it take Helen to plant 25 flowers?
a. 140 min
b. 120 min
c. 100 min
d. 80 min

Time

107. What time is shown on the clock below?

a. 12:00
b. 12:15
c. 2:00
d. 3:00

108. If Jake had to be at school at 9 o'clock A.M., and he arrived at 10:30 A.M., how many hours late is he?

a. $\frac{1}{2}$ an hour

b. 1 hour

c. $1\frac{1}{2}$ hours

d. 2 hours

109. If Sara quit working on her yard at 4:30 and she had been working for $2\frac{1}{2}$ hours, at what time did she start?

    a. 1:30

    b. 2:00

    c. 2:30

    d. 3:00

110. Jade went to see a movie. It started at 3:10 and ended at 5:30. How long was the movie?

    a. 1 hour and 20 minutes

    b. 1 hour and 40 minutes

    c. 2 hours and 40 minutes

    d. 2 hours and 20 minutes

111. What time does this clock show?

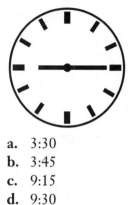

    a. 3:30

    b. 3:45

    c. 9:15

    d. 9:30

112. Tyson and LaDonna started swimming at 2:30 P.M. They stopped swimming at 4:45 P.M. Look at the clocks below.

How long did they swim?

    a. 2 hours, 30 minutes

    b. 2 hours, 15 minutes

    c. 1 hour, 45 minutes

    d. 1 hour, 15 minutes

Geometry

113. What is the name of the shape below?

    a. hexagon
    b. pentagon
    c. octagon
    d. square

114. What is the area of the rectangle? (Area = length × width)

8 feet

2 feet

    a. 8 feet
    b. 16 feet
    c. 4 feet
    d. 20 feet

115. What is the perimeter of the square?

6 feet

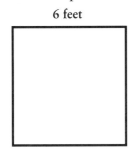

    a. 6 feet
    b. 12 feet
    c. 24 feet
    d. 36 feet

116. What is the perimeter of a square room if each side is 9 feet?
    a. 18 feet
    b. 27 feet
    c. 32 feet
    d. 36 feet

117. Which of the following is a parallelogram?

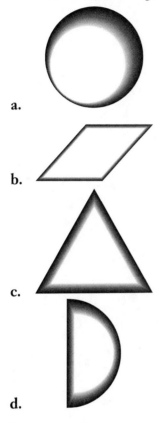

    a.

    b.

    c.

    d.

118. How many line segments are in the figure below?

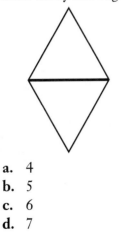

    a. 4
    b. 5
    c. 6
    d. 7

119. What is the name of the shape below?

    a. cylinder
    b. pentagon
    c. circle
    d. oval

120. Which shape has 2 lines of symmetry?

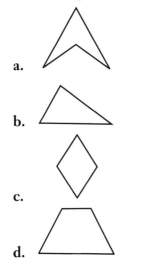

    a.

    b.

    c.

    d.

121. Which shape has more than 1 line of symmetry?

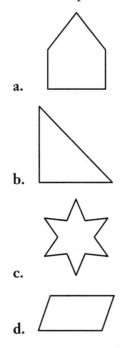

a.

b.

c.

d.

122. Which 2 figures are NOT congruent (same size, same shape)?

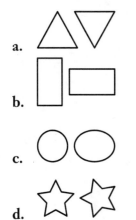

a.

b.

c.

d.

123. How many edges does a rectangular pyramid have?

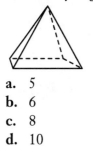

a. 5
b. 6
c. 8
d. 10

124. What is the *perimeter* of this rectangle?

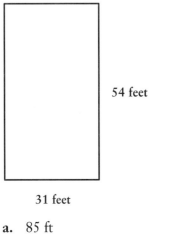

54 feet

31 feet

a. 85 ft
b. 116 ft
c. 139 ft
d. 170 ft

125. Which picture shows the diameter of a circle?

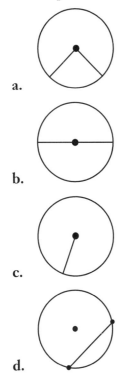

a.

b.

c.

d.

126. How many of these figures are NOT parallelograms?

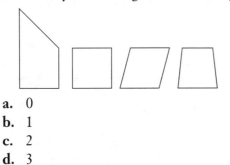

    a. 0
    b. 1
    c. 2
    d. 3

127. Which of these angles is an acute angle?

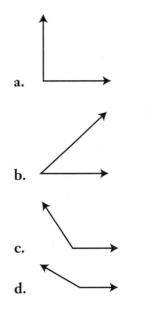

128. On the picture below, Jerris drew a line that was perpendicular to line P. Which picture below is Jerris's?

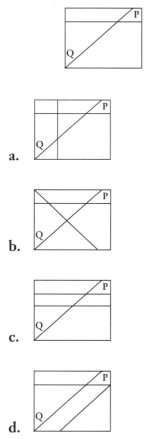

a.

b.

c.

d.

129. What is the area of the rectangle below?

8 ft

4 ft

a. 24 ft^3
b. 32 ft
c. 24 ft
d. 32 ft^2

130. Which of the pairs below is a pair of congruent figures?

a.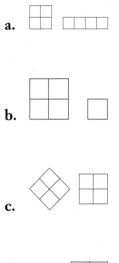

b.

c.

d.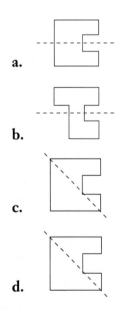

131. Which figure shows a line of symmetry?

a.

b.

c.

d.

132. A group of children used wire to make the rectangles shown. Each child used 24 inches of wire. Whose rectangle has the smallest area?

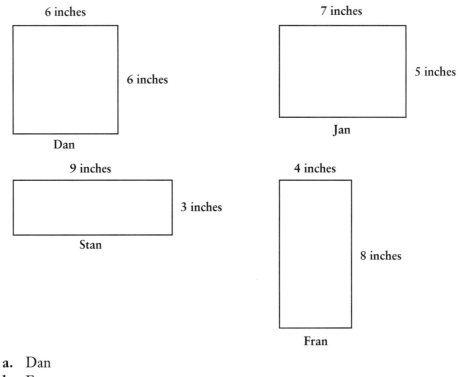

a. Dan
b. Fran
c. Jan
d. Stan

133. What is the area of this figure?

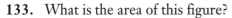
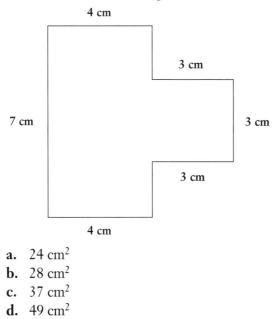

a. 24 cm²
b. 28 cm²
c. 37 cm²
d. 49 cm²

Number Concepts and Place Value

134. The Creston Bee Association counted the number of bees in several different hives at the start of each month. They counted 862 in May; 1,354 in June; 1,438 in July; and 1,329 in August. Which shows the number of bees counted in order from *greatest* to *least*?

a.	1,438	1,329	862	1,354
b.	1,354	1,329	1,438	862
c.	862	1,329	1,354	1,438
d.	1,438	1,354	1,329	862

135. What is the place value of the 8 in 381,513?
  a. Millions
  b. Hundred thousands
  c. Ten thousands
  d. Thousands

136. Which number is equal to six hundred eight thousand, nine hundred eighteen?
  a. 600,809,018
  b. 6,008,918
  c. 689,018
  d. 608,918

137. Olivia's ticket to the fair had an odd number on it. Which ticket could be Olivia's?

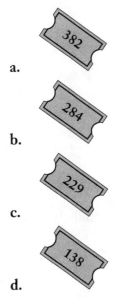

  a. 382

  b. 284

  c. 229

  d. 138

138. Which number has a 3 in the tenths place?
   a. 13.04
   b. 14.30
   c. 34.01
   d. 40.13

139. Which of the following numbers has an 8 in the hundreds place?
   a. 823,451
   b. 679,821
   c. 8,047,213
   d. 219.08

140. Which number sentence does NOT belong in the same fact family as the number sentence in the box?

$$\boxed{5 \times 4 = 20}$$

   a. $4 \times 5 = 20$
   b. $5 \div 4 = 1\frac{1}{4}$
   c. $20 \div 5 = 4$
   d. $20 \div 4 = 5$

141. This list shows the classroom numbers for the fifth grade teachers at Peach Grove Middle School next year.

Miss Chu	Room 12
Mrs. Dunn	Room 10
Mr. Farmer	Room 11
Mr. Greene	Room 9
Mrs. Wang	Room 8

Bobby looked at the list and said, "My classroom for next year has a prime number." Who will be Bobby's teacher next year?
   a. Mr. Farmer
   b. Miss Chu
   c. Mrs. Wang
   d. Mr. Greene

142. Three million, twenty-four thousand, eight hundred six candles were made by the Sweet Smells candle factory during the last five years. Which number below shows the number of candles made?
   a. 32,486
   b. 3,024,806
   c. 3,024,860
   d. 3,248,006

143. According to the commutative property of multiplication, which statement below is true?
   a. $3 \times 2 = 2 \times 3$
   b. $(3 \times 2) \times 4 = 3 \times (2 \times 4)$
   c. $3 \times 0 = 0$
   d. $3 \times 1 = 3$

144. Which group of numbers is in the correct order from smallest to largest? You may use the number line below to help answer the question.

   a. $\frac{9}{4}$ 2.15 $2\frac{3}{4}$
   b. $\frac{9}{4}$ $2\frac{3}{4}$ 2.15
   c. 2.15 $2\frac{3}{4}$ $\frac{9}{4}$
   d. 2.15 $\frac{9}{4}$ $2\frac{3}{4}$

145. $(-3) + (-8) =$
   a. -5
   b. 5
   c. -11
   d. 11

146. Which of the expressions below does NOT have the same value as the others?
   a. $2 \times 2 \times 25$
   b. $4 \times 5 \times 10$
   c. 5×20
   d. 10×10

147. This picture shows the kinds of juice and fruit in Pedro's kitchen. How many different ways can Pedro choose one kind of juice and one kind of fruit to put in his lunch?

a. 3
b. 6
c. 9
d. 12

148. What does the 2 represent in the number 1,423,013?
    a. 2 thousands
    b. 2 millions
    c. 2 tens
    d. 2 ten-thousands

149. Maria's family is planning a camping trip at the beach. The chart below shows the distance from Maria's home city to several beach campgrounds. The campgrounds are listed in alphabetical order. Which campground is FARTHEST from where Maria lives?

DISTANCE TO CAMPGROUNDS	
Name of Campground	Distance in Miles
Nokomis	159.9
Osprey	161.3
Palm Bay	151.4
Venice	161.1

a. Nokomis
b. Osprey
c. Palm Bay
d. Venice

150. Which number is in the hundreds place in the number 675,324?
   a. 5
   b. 3
   c. 2
   d. 4

151. Which number is in the tenths place in the number 968.73?
   a. 6
   b. 8
   c. 7
   d. 3

Algebra

152. Each symbol in the number sentences below has a specific value.

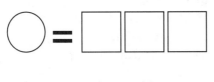

Study the first two sentences, then choose the answer that best finishes the last sentence.

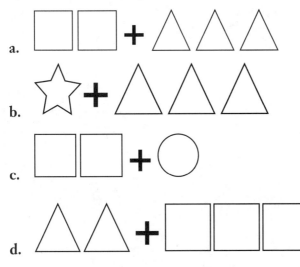

a.

b.

c.

d.

153. Which number sentence is in the same family of facts as $4 \times 9 = 36$?
   a. $36 - 4 = 32$
   b. $4 + 9 = 13$
   c. $6 \times 6 = 36$
   d. $\frac{36}{9} = 4$

154. There are 8 pieces of candy in a jar. Each piece of candy is either chocolate or fruit. Without looking, Regive picked a piece of candy out of the jar. He recorded the type of candy and placed it back in the jar. He did this 16 times. The chart below shows his results.

FRUIT	CHOCOLATE
11	5

From these results, which statement would most likely be true?

   a. There are more chocolate candies than fruit candies.
   b. There are the same number of chocolate and fruit candies.
   c. There are more fruit candies than chocolate candies.
   d. There are twice as many chocolate candies as fruit candies

155. Which number sentence is in the same family of facts as $\frac{15}{5} = 3$?
   a. $15 - 5 = 10$
   b. $5 \times 3 = 15$
   c. $5 + 3 = 8$
   d. $15 \times 3 = 45$

156. Which number should be placed in the box below to make the equation true?
   $68 - \boxed{} = 41$
   a. 27
   b. 41
   c. 68
   d. 109

157. Find the value of y if $y = 16 - x$ and $x = 7$.
   a. 23
   b. 16
   c. 9
   d. 7

Logic

158. Each student in Miss King's class is going to decorate a picture frame with seashells. Miss King says there will be enough shells if each student uses 18 shells. What else do you need to know to find out how many seashells there are in all?

    a. the size of the picture frames
    b. the number of shells in a bag
    c. the number of students in the class
    d. the size of the shells

159. Mr. Wilson wants to know how many buses to request for the 4th grade field trip to the zoo. How should he find the number of buses needed?

    a. multiply the number of people by the number of seats in a bus
    b. add the number of people to the number of seats in a bus
    c. divide the number of seats on a bus by the number of people
    d. divide the number of people by the number of seats on a bus

160. Which figure could be turned clockwise or counterclockwise so it would look just like the figure below?

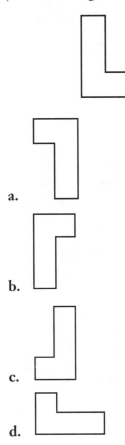

    a.

    b.

    c.

    d.

Mathematical Representation

161. Richard babysat for 17 hours per week for 6 weeks. Which sentence could be used to find the total number of hours he babysat?

a. $\dfrac{17}{\text{total number of hours}} = 6$

b. $17 - 6 = (\text{total number of hours})$

c. $(\text{total number of hours}) + 6 = 17$

d. $17 \times 6 = (\text{total number of hours})$

162. Justine read 13 books during summer vacation. Her sister, Lamilah, read twice as many books as Justine. Which sentence could be used to find the number of books Lamilah read?

a. $13 + 2 = (\text{number of books Lamiliah read})$

b. $(\text{number of books Lamiliah read}) - 13 = 2$

c. $\dfrac{13}{\text{number of books Lamiliah read}} = 2$

d. $13 \times 2 = (\text{number of books Lamiliah read})$

163. For 140 minutes, Shanthi raked leaves, filling 7 bags. Which sentence could be used to find out how long it took to fill each bag?

a. $7 \times 140 = (\text{number of minutes to fill each bag})$

b. $\dfrac{140}{7} = (\text{number of minutes to fill each bag})$

c. $(\text{number of minutes to fill each bag}) + 140 = 7$

d. $140 - (\text{number of minutes to fill each bag}) = 7$

164. Akiko was selling lemonade. She started with 14 glasses of lemonade, but after 42 minutes she only had 3 left. Which shows the number of glasses Akiko sold in 42 minutes?

a. $\dfrac{42}{14}$

b. $42 + 3 - 14$

c. $14 - 3$

d. $42 - 3$

Order of Operations

165. $3 \times (2 + 4) - 1 =$
    a. 17
    b. 15
    c. 14
    d. 9

166. $(3 \times 6) - (4 \div 2) =$
    a. 3
    b. 7
    c. 12
    d. 16

167. $8 + 9 \div 3 - 4 + 2$
    a. $(8 + 9) \div 3 - 4 + 2$
    b. $(8 + 9) \div (3 - 4) + 2$
    c. $8 + (9 \div 3) - 4 + 2$
    d. $8 + 9 \div 3 - (4 + 2)$

168. $(18 - 6) \div (2 + 4) =$
    a. 2
    b. 10
    c. 17
    d. 19

Probability and Statistics

169. Bridget picked 1 pen from each of 2 jars. The first jar had only blue and black pens. The second had only red and yellow pens. Which 2 pens could Bridget have picked?
    a. 1 red, 1 yellow
    b. 1 blue, 1 black
    c. 2 blue
    d. 1 yellow, 1 blue

170. Yamil has 19 paperclips in a jar. There are 4 paperclips that are red, 3 that are yellow, 7 that are green, and 5 that are silver. If Yamil reaches into the jar and takes out 1 paperclip, which color will it *most likely* be?
    a. Red
    b. Yellow
    c. Green
    d. Silver

171. Biliana is packing for a trip. Of her 3 striped and 5 solid shirts, she is going to take 4 shirts. Which is NOT a possible outcome for the 4 shirts she packs?

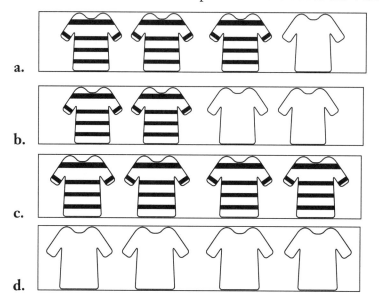

a.

b.

c.

d.

172. Debra will choose one of these buttons without looking.

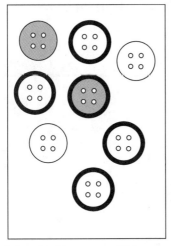

Which kind of button will it most likely be?

a.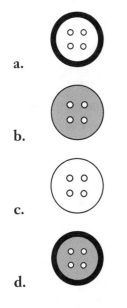

b.

c.

d.

173. The spinner below was used by students for an experiment. What is the probability that the spinner will stop on a number greater than 6?

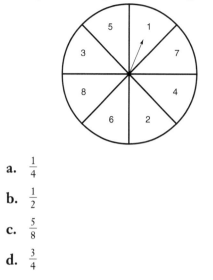

a. $\frac{1}{4}$

b. $\frac{1}{2}$

c. $\frac{5}{8}$

d. $\frac{3}{4}$

Measurement

174. Mila wants to walk all the way around her block. If each side is 110 meters long and Mila starts and stops at her house, how far will she have walked?

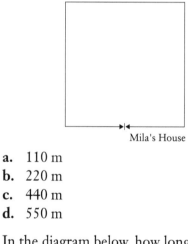

Mila's House

a. 110 m
b. 220 m
c. 440 m
d. 550 m

175. In the diagram below, how long is the crayon?

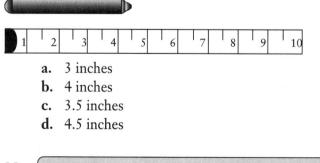

a. 3 inches
b. 4 inches
c. 3.5 inches
d. 4.5 inches

176. Veronica is wrapping a package and wants to tie a ribbon around it. Which of the following instruments could she use to measure how much ribbon she needs?

a.
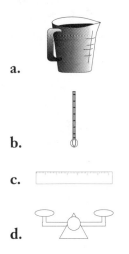

b.

c.

d.

Graphs and Charts

For questions 177 and 178, please use the following graph.

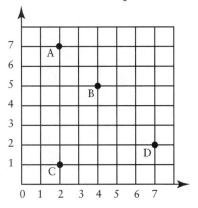

177. From (2,4) Juan walked, in a straight line, up 3 blocks. Where did he stop? (Each square in the grid above represents one block).

a. A
b. B
c. C
d. D

178. Tina walked in a straight line from (7,6) to (3,6). How far did she walk?

    a. 3 blocks

    b. 4 blocks

    c. 5 blocks

    d. 6 blocks

179. Which grid below shows $y = 2x$?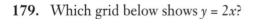

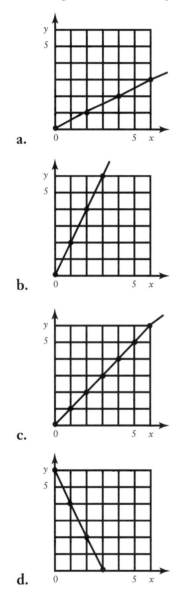

    a.

    b.

    c.

    d.

180. The graph shows the types of music and the number of CDs that Libby and Matt have.

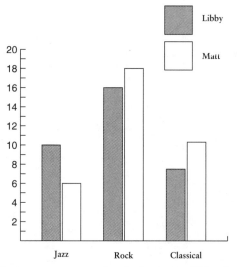

How many more classical music CDs does Matt have than Libby?
a. 18
b. 6
c. 4
d. 3

181. The screen below shows the mixed-up high scores of several students for a computer game. Who really had the *second* highest score?

MATH BLASTER
HIGH SCORES

1. Beth	2,421
2. Darin	2,521
3. Elva	3,421
4. Ben	3,086
5. Chad	3,488
6. Darla	2,999

a. Beth
b. Darin
c. Darla
d. Elva

182. The tally chart below shows the hair color of the students in Miss Kim's class. How many students are in Miss Kim's class?

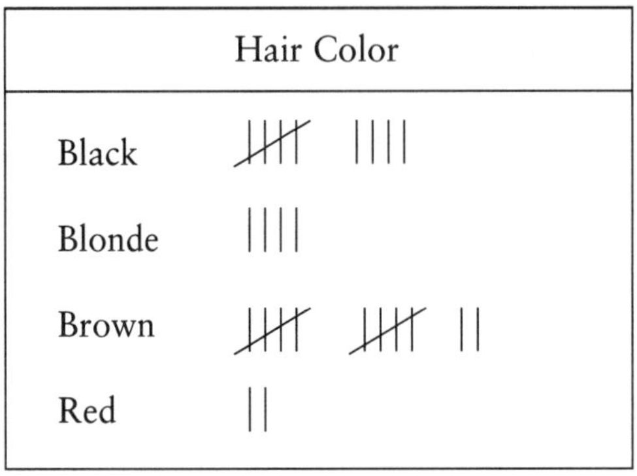

Hair Color	
Black	ЍꞱ ||||
Blonde	||||
Brown	ЍꞱ ЍꞱ ||
Red	||

  a. 4
  b. 15
  c. 24
  d. 27

Use the graph below for questions 183 and 184.

The graph shows the number of dogs groomed during one week at Pretty Dog Salon.

Dogs Groomed at
Pretty Dog Salon

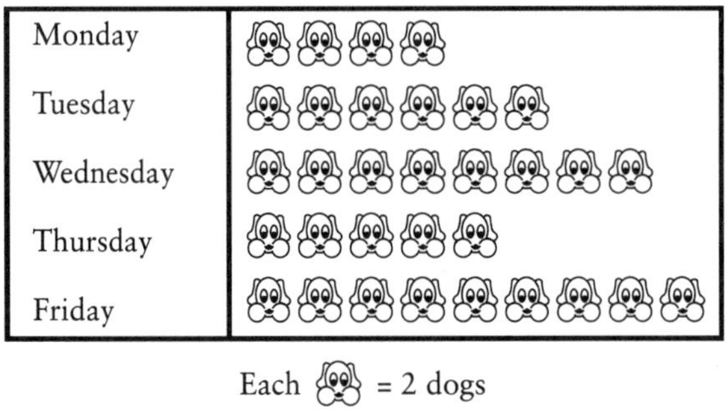

Monday	🐶🐶🐶🐶
Tuesday	🐶🐶🐶🐶🐶🐶
Wednesday	🐶🐶🐶🐶🐶🐶🐶🐶
Thursday	🐶🐶🐶🐶🐶
Friday	🐶🐶🐶🐶🐶🐶🐶🐶🐶

Each 🐶 = 2 dogs

183. On how many days were more than 8 dogs groomed?
  a. 1
  b. 2
  c. 3
  d. 4

184. How many more dogs were groomed on Friday than on Tuesday?
  a. 3
  b. 4
  c. 6
  d. 8

185. This table shows the measurements of rectangular gardens planted by three friends. The friends are planning to build fences around their gardens. Fence boards are one foot wide. Who will need to buy the largest number of boards to put around his garden?

Name	Width (feet)	Length (feet)	Area (square feet)
Abel	4	9	36
Joseph	6	6	36
Ned	3	12	36

   a. Abel
   b. Joseph
   c. Ned
   d. They all need the same number of boards.

186. The chart below shows the number of books read during May by several students. Which students read a prime number of books?

BOOKS READ IN MAY	
Abby	4
Dale	3
Gwen	2
Jake	5
Noel	6
Rilla	9

   a. Abby, Dale, Jake
   b. Abby, Gwen, Noel
   c. Dale, Gwen, Jake
   d. Only Rilla

Answers

1. **b.** First do what is in the parentheses, $3 + 5 = 8$, and then $8 + 6 = 14$.
2. **b.** $11 + 3 = 14$, and $14 + 7 = 21$
3. **c.** *Altogether* is a code word for *add them up*. $651 + 491 + 537 = 1{,}679$
4. **c.** $57 + 36 + 43 + 35 = 171$
5. **a.** This is simply asking you to add all the numbers up. When you see the word *sum*, think *add*.
6. **a.** $(8{,}964 + 2{,}876) = 11{,}840$. Add that to $1{,}123$ to get $12{,}963$.
7. **b.** This is a simple addition problem. $347 + 287 = 661$.
8. **c.** *Altogether* means *add*: $470 + 590 = 1{,}060$.
9. **d.** $279 + 68 = 347$. If you chose another answer, watch out for careless mistakes.
10. **b.** $1{,}102 + 1{,}158 + 967 = 3{,}227$
11. **b.** $738 - 193 = 545$
12. **c.** $24 - 5 = 19$
13. **d.** $4{,}321 - 1{,}234 = 3{,}087$
14. **d.** $10{,}702 - 9{,}381 = 1{,}321$
15. **a.** Subtract: $832 - 63 = 769$.
16. **b.** Subtract Betty's score from the highest score ever made to get the answer: $9{,}689 - 6{,}752 = 2{,}937$.
17. **a.** $805 - 382 = 423$. Again, if you chose another answer, you may have made a careless mistake.
18. **c.** 2 party favors $\times$ 15 friends = 30 party favors, and 5 lollipops $\times$ 15 friends equals 75 lollipops.
19. **a.** $(4 \times 4) = 16$ and $(3 \times 3) = 9$. Then add $16 + 9$ to get 25.
20. **b.** $(7 \times 8) = 56$ and $56 - 14 = 42$.
21. **d.** $(6 \times 8) = 48$ and $(3 \times 4) = 12$. Finally, $48 - 12 = 36$.
22. **b.** 5 yards times 4 sides (because a square has 4 sides) equals 20.
23. **b.** $7 \times 4 = 28$, and $28 + 43 = 71$.
24. **b.** If he has 34 chickens and each one lays 27 eggs per day, that is 34×27, which is 918. Then you have to multiply by 7 to find one full weeks' worth. $918 \times 7 = 6{,}426$. If you picked answer **a**, you forgot to multiply for the week.
25. **c.** 98 pages multiplied by 3 minutes per page equals 294 minutes.
26. **d.** 17 times 38 equals 646.
27. **c.** $234 \times 51 = 11{,}934$.
28. **a.** $264 \times 437 = 115{,}368$.
29. **b.** 24 cookies times 7 chips in each equals 168.
30. **c.** 54 bags times 8 pieces in each equals 432.
31. **c.** $34 \times 21 = 714$.
32. **c.** $28 \times 13 = 364$.
33. **d.** This is a multiplication problem. $15 \times 23 = 345$. If you picked answer **a**, you added instead of multiplied.
34. **b.** $539 \times 62 = 33{,}418$.

35. **c.** $3 \times 285 = 855$.
36. **b.** This is a multiplication problem. 34 miles times 27 gallons $= 34 \times 27 = 918$.
37. **c.** This question is asking you to multiply 16 by 24. $16 \times 24 = 384$.
38. **d.** For this question you have to multiply 17 times 675, which equals 11,475.
39. **d.** $64 \div 4 = 16$. If you want to check your work, 16×4 does equal 64.
40. **c.** This question is asking you to divide 8 slices by 2 kids, and $8 \div 2 = 4$.
41. **d.** $63 \div 7 = 9$.
42. **b.** $82 \div 9 = 9$ with a remainder of 1. $(9 \times 9 = 81)$.
43. **b.** $16 \div 4 = 4$, and $4 + 3 = 7$.
44. **a.** $42 \div 6 = 7$, and $7 - 5 = 2$.
45. **d.** $27 \div 3 = 9$, and $9 + 4 = 13$.
46. **a.** 378 CDs $\div$ 7 sold per day equals 54 days to sell them all.
47. **d.** 2,442 dolls $\div$ 6 per box equals 407 boxes needed.
48. **a.** 2,520 books $\div$ 60 per shelf equals 42 shelves.
49. **c.** $874 \div 8 = 109$ with a remainder of 2.
50. **d.** $720 \div 20$ equals 36.
51. **b.** $225 \div 25 = 9$.
52. **d.** $74 \div 8 = 9$ with a remainder of 2. This is because 8 goes into 74 nine times $(8 \times 9 = 72)$ and there are 2 left over, because $74 - 72 = 2$.
53. **c.** This is a division problem. If there are 72 trees, you divide by 12 rows to find the number in each row. $72 \div 12 = 6$.
54. **b.** If there are 49 cookies and 7 people, $49 \div 7 = 7$ cookies each.
55. **d.** $70 \div 9 = 7$ with a remainder of 7. This is because 9 goes into 70 seven times $(9 \times 7 = 63)$ and there are 7 left over, because $70 - 63 = 7$.
56. **c.** $167 \div 7 = 23$ with a remainder of 6. This is because 7 goes into 167 twenty-three times $(7 \times 23 = 161)$ and there are 6 left over, because $167 - 161 = 6$.
57. **d.** $69 \div 4 = 17$ with a remainder of 1. This is because 4 goes into 69 seventeen times $(4 \times 17 = 68)$ and there is 1 left over, because $69 - 68 = 1$.
58. **c.** This is a division problem. 588 beads divided between 6 bracelets equals 98.
59. **b.** 420 towels divided by 12 boxes equals 35 towels per box.
60. **b.** First add 364 and 241 to get 605 fish. Then subtract: $605 - 123 = 482$. If you chose answer **a**, you forgot to subtract.
61. **c.** First add up what she spent: $4 + 2 + 3 = 9$. Then subtract from the original amount: $16 - 9 = 7$.
62. **d.** First, multiply 4 cookies by 2 girls to get 8 cookies. Then multiply 6 cookies by 3 kids to get 18. Then add them together: $8 + 18 = 26$.
63. **a.** First add to figure out how many nails she has: $23 + 17 = 40$. Then subtract to find out how many more she needs: $60 - 40 = 20$.
64. **a.** Finding the product means multiplying, and $93 \times 84 = 7,812$. Then add 7,812 plus 171 to get 7,983.
65. **d.** First subtract: $492 - 233 = 259$. Then add the new ones he bought: $259 + 42 = 301$.

66. **b.** She starts out with $437. She writes 2 checks for $42 and $59, for a total of $101. Subtract: $437 - 101 = 336$.

67. **a.** This question may seem harder than it actually is because they give you extra information that you don't need. Ben started with 26 books and had 21 left. $26 - 21 = 5$.

68. **a.** If he needed 7 gallons for the first half, then he would need 7 gallons for the second half. If he used 2, then all he would need now is $7 - 2$.

69. **b.** Bricks are only sold in groups of 25, so that rules out answers **a** and **c** because they are not divisible by 25. $25 \times 6 = 150$, and $25 \times 7 = 175$. You would have enough bricks by buying only 150, so the correct answer is **b**.

70. **b.** For this question, first you have to figure out how many stickers he wants to give to his cousins, which would be $132 - 42 = 90$, (because he has 132 and wants to keep 42). Then, you divide 90 by 6, which equals 15.

71. **d.** First add up the cards Dulce got rid of: $207 + 18 = 225$. Then you subtract that from the original amount, which is $872 - 225 = 647$, to find out how many she had left.

72. **d.** $12.53 rounded to the nearest dollar is $13. Answer **c** is not to the nearest dollar. If the amount of cents is over 50, you have to round up, so it is not answer **b**. And answer **a** is to the nearest ten dollars, not the nearest dollar.

73. **b.** 51,471 rounds down to the nearest thousand: 51,000.

74. **c.** First figure out about how many times he went down the hill: $37 \times 4 = 148$, which is between 125 and 175.

75. **c.** First figure out how many animals were on the farm: $23 + 49 + 68 = 140$, which is between 120 and 180.

76. **c.** First multiply 347×7 days in one week, to get 2,429. Of the answer choices, 2,450 is by far the closest.

77. **b.** First figure out how much more money he needs: $9,460 - 4,950 = 4,510$. That number is between $4,200 and $4,700.

78. **a.** 43 rounds to 40 and 31 rounds to 30; $40 + 30 = 70$.

79. **a.** 498 rounds to 500 and 211 rounds to 200; $500 + 200 = 700$.

80. **a.** 328 rounds to 300 and 451 rounds to 500; $300 + 500 = 800$.

81. **d.** 2,904 rounds to 3,000, and 3,210 also rounds to 3,000. $3,000 + 3,000 = 6,000$.

82. **a.** $3.29 + 3.29 + 6.49 = 13.07$.

83. **b.** $2.5 + 1.25 + 1.35 = 5.1$. When figuring out this question, make sure you line up the decimal points correctly. If you picked answer **c** you probably didn't line up your decimal points properly.

84. **a.** $20 is the same as 20.00. Subtract: $20.00 - 8.97 = 11.03$.

85. **b.** $9.1 + 8.7 + 7.3 + 6.4 = 31.5$ total gallons.

86. **c.** $3.2 + 4.5 + 10 = 17.7$. Make sure you line up your decimal points correctly.

87. **c.** $4.3 \times 5.2 = 22.36$.

88. **d.** $7.4 - 3.9 = 3.5$.

89. **c.** This is just basic subtraction with decimals. $17.34 - 9.18 = 8.16$.

90. **b.** When you are asked to find the product, you are being asked to multiply. $1.8 \times 7.6 = 13.68$.

91. **a.** This question is asking you to add the numbers together, and $88.23 + 91.05 + 75.46 = 254.74$.

92. **b.** Subtract: $3\frac{2}{5} - 1\frac{1}{5} = 2\frac{1}{5}$ yards.

93. **c.** $\frac{1}{7} + \frac{3}{7} = \frac{4}{7}$.

94. **b.** $\frac{3}{10} + \frac{6}{10} = \frac{9}{10}$.

95. **d.** $6\frac{3}{4} - 4\frac{1}{4} = 2\frac{1}{2}$.

96. **c.** $3\frac{1}{2} + 4\frac{1}{2} = 8$.

97. **a.** $\frac{1}{2}$ of the oval is shaded.

98. **b.** 7 out of 8 of the boxes are shaded, so the answer is $\frac{7}{8}$.

99. **c.** Pie **c** shows $\frac{1}{2}$ of an eaten pie.

100. **a.** Answer **a** shows 4 out of 7 apples shaded, or $\frac{4}{7}$.

101. **c.** There are 12 stickers altogether, and 5 of them are hearts, so the answer is $\frac{5}{12}$.

102. **b.** This pattern is simply counting by threes, so the next number is 15.

103. **c.** This pattern is counting by twos. Two hours after 5 o'clock is 7 o'clock.

104. **a.** The next shape in the pattern is the rectangle.

105. **c.** This pattern is increasing by 3, so the answer is $16 + 3 = 19$.

106. **c.** The number of minutes is four times the number of flowers, so it should take her 25×4 minutes to plant 25 flowers, or 100 minutes.

107. **d.** The time shown is 3 o'clock.

108. **c.** 10:30 is one hour and 30 minutes after 9:00, so the answer is $1\frac{1}{2}$ hours.

109. **b.** 4:30 is $2\frac{1}{2}$ hours after 2:00.

110. **d.** There are two hours and twenty minutes between 3:10 and 5:30.

111. **c.** In this picture, the little hand is on the 9 and the big hand is on the 3, showing 9:15.

112. **b.** The first clock shows 2:30 and the second clock shows 4:45. The difference between the two is 2 hours and 15 minutes.

113. **a.** A two-dimensional figure with 6 sides is called a hexagon. A pentagon has 5 sides, an octagon has 8 sides, and a square has 4 sides.

114. **b.** The question tells you that area = length × width, so multiply $8 \times 2 = 16$.

115. **c.** To find the perimeter, you have to add up all the sides. Since all the sides of a square are the same length, the answer is $6 + 6 + 6 + 6 = 24$.

116. **d.** Again, you must add up all the sides to find the perimeter. $9 + 9 + 9 + 9 = 36$ (or $9 \times 4 = 36$).

117. **b.** Figure **a** is a circle, figure **b** is a parallelogram, figure **c** is a triangle and figure **d** is a half of a circle.

118. **b.** There are 5 line segments.

119. **a.** The shape is a cylinder.

120. **c.** The diamond shows two lines of symmetry, one down the middle and one straight across.

121. **c.** The star has many lines of symmetry. All the other figures only have one line of symmetry.

122. **c.** The circle and the oval are different shapes and different sizes. The triangles are the same except one is upside down; the rectangles are the same except one is going up and down and one is on its side; and the stars are the same except one is tilted.

123. **c.** If you count the edges in the picture, you will see that there are 8.

124. **d.** To find the perimeter, you add up all the sides of the figure, in this case: $54 + 54 + 31 + 31 = 170$.

125. **b.** The diameter cuts directly across the center of a circle, in this case it is figure **b**. If you picked answer **c**, that is the radius.

126. **c.** The first and last are not parallelograms.

127. **b.** An acute angle is less than 90 degrees. Answer **a** shows a right angle, and answers **c** and **d** show obtuse angles.

128. **a.** This question is a bit tricky. Ignore line "Q" and just look at line "P." Answer **a** shows a line drawn at a 90 degree angle to "P," which is perpendicular. Answer **b** shows a line drawn perpendicular to "Q" and answer **c** shows a line drawn parallel to "P." Lastly, answer **d** shows a line drawn parallel to "Q."

129. **d.** Area is simply length × width, in this case $8 \times 4 = 32$.

130. **c.** Congruent means the same size and the same shape. The only answer choice that fits this definition is answer c.

131. **a.** A line of symmetry is one where the figure can be flipped over and still look the same on both sides. That is figure **a**.

132. **d.** Dan's rectangle has an area of 6×6, which is 36. Fran's rectangle has an area of 4×8, which is 32. Jan's rectangle has an area of 7×5, which is 35. But Stan's rectangle has an area of 9×3, which is 27, the smallest area shown.

133. **c.** For this question, it is best to break the figure down into 2 smaller shapes: the first one is a square with a side of 3, and the second shape is a rectangle with a length of 7 and a width of 4. Then, just find the areas and add them together. $3 \times 3 = 9$, and $7 \times 4 = 28$, and lastly $9 + 28 = 37$.

134. **d.** This answer shows the numbers in order from greatest to least. Answer **c** shows the numbers in order from least to greatest.

135. **c.** The number 8 is in the ten-thousands place.

136. **d.** Answer **a** is equal to six hundred million, eight hundred nine thousand, eighteen. Answer **b** is equal to six million, eight thousand, nine hundred eighteen. Answer **c** is equal to six hundred eighty nine thousand, eighteen.

137. **c.** Any number that ends with a 1, 3, 5, 7, or 9 is an odd number. Any number that ends with a 0, 2, 4, 6, or 8 is an even number. Her number was an odd number; the only odd number shown is answer **c**.

138. **b.** Choice **b** has the 3 in the tenths place. Choice **a** has the 3 in the ones place, choice **c** has the 3 in the tens place and choice **d** has the 3 in the hundredths place.

139. **b.** In the number 679,821, the 8 is in the hundreds place. In choice **a**, the 8 is in the hundred thousands place. In choice **c**, the 8 is in the millions place. And in answer choice **d**, the 8 is in the *hundredths* place.

140. **b.** For answer choices **a**, **c**, and **d**, the basic fact you have to know is $5 \times 4 = 20$. Answer **b** does not show this fact.

141. **a.** A prime number is a number that can only be divided evenly by the number one and itself. Twelve can be divided by 1, 2, 3, 4, 6, and 12. Ten can be divided by 1, 2, 5, and 10. Nine can be divided by 1, 3, and 9. Eight can be divided by 1, 2, 4, and 8. But 11 can only be divided by 1 and 11, so it is a prime number. Mr. Farmer is in room 11.

142. **b.** Answer **a** shows the number thirty-two thousand, four hundred eighty-six. Answer **c** shows the number three million, twenty-four thousand, eight hundred sixty. Answer **d** shows the number three million, two hundred forty-eight thousand, six. Only answer **b** shows the number three million, twenty-four thousand, eight hundred six.

143. **a.** The commutative property is $a + b = b + a$, or $a \times b = b \times a$. If you picked answer **b**, you picked the associative property. The associative property is $(a + b) + c = a + (b + c)$ or $(a \times b) \times c = a \times (b \times c)$.

144. **d.** In answer **a**, $\frac{9}{4}$ is the same as 2.25, which is more than 2.15, so that is incorrect. In answer **b**, $\frac{9}{4}$ (or 2.25) and $2\frac{3}{4}$ (or 2.75) are both larger than 2.15. And in answer **c**, $2\frac{3}{4}$ (or 2.75) is larger than $\frac{9}{4}$ (or 2.25), so the only correct answer is **d**. 2.15 is smaller than $\frac{9}{4}$ (or 2.25), which is smaller than $2\frac{3}{4}$ (or 2.75).

145. **c.** A negative number plus a negative number gives you a negative number. $(-3) + (-8) = (-11)$.

146. **b.** $2 \times 2 \times 25 = 100$, $4 \times 5 \times 10 = 200$, $5 \times 20 = 100$ and $10 \times 10 = 100$, so the correct answer is **b**.

147. **c.** He can choose apple juice with a banana, apple juice with grapes, or apple juice with a pear for 3 different choices. He can choose fruit punch with a banana, fruit punch with grapes or fruit punch with a pear for 3 more choices. And he can choose orange juice with a banana, orange with grapes or orange with a pear for 3 more choices. $3 + 3 + 3 = 9$ choices altogether.

148. **d.** The two is in the ten thousands place. (The number 3 is in the thousands place, the number 1 is in the millions, place and the number 1 is also in the tens place.)

149. **b.** For this question, you just have to see which one has the biggest number; in this case it is 161.3, which is *Osprey*.

150. **b.** 3 is in the hundreds place, 5 is in the thousands place, 2 is in the tens and 4 is in the ones.

151. **c.** 7 is in the *tenths* place, 6 is in the *tens*. 8 is in the ones and 3 is in the hundredths.

152. **d.** If the circle is the same as 3 squares, and the star is the same as 2 triangles, then a circle plus a star is the same as 3 squares plus 2 triangles. Choice **d** is the only one that shows this.

153. **d.** This is the only answer choice that is showing the same numbers, and the underlying fact you must know is $4 \times 9 = 36$, because $36 \div 9 = 4$.

154. **c.** Based on the information given, it is safe to assume that there are probably more fruit candies than chocolate candies, since he picked a fruit candy more than twice as many times as he picked a chocolate candy.

155. **b.** This is the only answer choice that is showing the same numbers, and the underlying fact you must know is $5 \times 3 = 15$, and $15 \div 5 = 3$.

156. **a.** $68 - 27 = 41$. We know this because $68 - 41 = 27$.

157. **c.** For this question, you have to substitute 7 for x, making the equation $y = 16 - 7$, or $y = 9$.

158. **c.** To find out how many shells there are in all, you would multiply 18 times the number of students in the class. It doesn't matter what size the picture frames are, the number of shells in a bag, or the size of the shells.

159. **d.** To find the number of buses needed, you would divide the number of people by the number of seats on a bus.

160. **a.** Only this figure could be turned clockwise or counterclockwise to look just like the figure above.

161. **d.** To find the total number of hours he babysat, you would multiply 17×6, as shown in answer **d**.

162. **d.** To find the number of books Lamiliah read, you would multiply 13×2, as shown in choice **d**.

163. **b.** To find out how long it took to fill each bag, you would divide 140 by 7, as shown in choice **b**.

164. **c.** $14 - 3$ would tell you how many she already sold.

165. **a.** You must do what is in the parentheses first. $2 + 4 = 6$, and $3 \times 6 = 18$, and $18 - 1 = 17$. You can remember this mnemonic device to learn the order of operations: **Please Excuse My Dear Aunt Sally.** It tells you to first do the **p**arentheses, then **e**xponents, **m**ultiplication, **d**ivision, **a**ddition, and then **s**ubtraction, in that order. If you picked answer **d**, you ignored the parentheses and just did the math going straight across.

166. **d.** Remember, do what is in the parentheses first: $(3 \times 6) = 18$ and $(4 \div 2) = 2$. Lastly $18 - 2 = 16$.

167. **c.** This question is testing whether you know the order of operations: first do the parentheses, then exponents, multiplication, division, addition and then subtraction. Answer **c** shows that you should do the division before the addition and subtraction.

168. **a.** $(18 - 6) = 12$ and $(2 + 4) = 6$. Then you figure out $12 \div 6 = 2$.

169. **d.** It cannot be answer **a** because that would mean she only picked from the second jar. It cannot be answer **b** because that would mean she only picked from

the first jar. It cannot be answer **c** because that would mean she only picked from the first jar. It can only be answer **d**.

170. **c.** The chance of picking a green one is $\frac{7}{19}$. The chance of picking a red one is $\frac{4}{19}$, a yellow one is $\frac{3}{19}$, and a silver one is $\frac{5}{19}$. Since you have the greatest chance of picking a green paperclip, that is the color it will most likely be.

171. **c.** It cannot have this outcome because she does not have 4 striped shirts, she only has 3.

172. **a.** The chance she will pick this button is $\frac{4}{8}$. The chance she would pick the button in choice **b** is $\frac{1}{8}$, the chance she would pick the button in choice **c** is $\frac{2}{8}$, and the chance she would pick the button in choice **d** is $\frac{1}{8}$. That means she has the greatest chance of picking the button from choice **a**.

173. **a.** It has a $\frac{2}{8}$ chance of landing on a number greater than 6 (in other words 7 or 8). $\frac{2}{8}$ is the same as $\frac{1}{4}$.

174. **c.** If you look closely, walking completely around the block is the same as finding the perimeter. If each side is 110, just add up the sides: $110 + 110 + 110 + 110 = 440$.

175. **d.** The crayon measures 4.5 inches.

176. **c.** This question has an obvious answer: To measure a ribbon, you would use a ruler.

177. **a.** If he started at (2,4) and walked up three blocks, he would end at (2,7), which is point A.

178. **b.** She walked 4 blocks.

179. **b.** Graph B plots the line of $y = 2x$. It shows the points (0,0), (1,2), (2,4) and (3,6).

180. **c.** If you look at the graph, you would see that Matt has 11 classical CDs and Libby has 7. $11 - 7 = 4$.

181. **d.** Ben scored 3,086 and Chad scored 3,488. Elva scored 3,421, which is more than Ben but less than Chad.

182. **d.** If you count up all the tally marks, you would see that it is equal to 27.

183. **d.** Remember, each picture equals 2 dogs. There were 12 dogs groomed on Tuesday, 16 dogs groomed on Wednesday, 10 dogs groomed on Thursday, and 18 dogs groomed on Friday.

184. **c.** There were 12 dogs groomed on Tuesday, and 18 dogs groomed on Friday. $18 - 12 = 6$. If you picked answer **a**, you forgot that one picture of a dog equals 2 dogs.

185. **c.** This question is tricky because while you are given the area, what you really need is the perimeter for each one. The perimeter for Abel's is $4 + 4 + 9 + 9 = 26$. The perimeter for Joseph's is $6 + 6 + 6 + 6 = 24$. The perimeter for Ned's is $3 + 3 + 12 + 12 = 30$, so he would need the most boards. If you picked answer **d**, you just looked at the areas instead of finding the perimeters.

186. **c.** A prime number is a number that can only be divided evenly by the number one and itself. 2, 3, and 5 are prime numbers. 4 can be divided by 1, 2 and 4. Six can be divided by 1, 2, 3 and 6. And 9 can be divided by 1, 3, and 9.

CHAPTER

Open-Ended Math Questions

Most state assessment tests ask you to solve open-ended math questions. Simply put, this means that the questions you answer require you to explain how you solved the problem by showing all the calculations. If you get the right answer, but fail to show your work, you will not be given full credit. In fact, you can actually receive the same score for a question—when you give only the correct answer—as someone who got the wrong answer but showed all his or her work.

You will find a page of *Pattern Blocks* on the next page. Some of the questions will ask you to use this to help solve problems.

This page can be photocopied in order to make pattern block cutouts. Copy this page and cut out the shapes. Use them to complete the design on page 73.

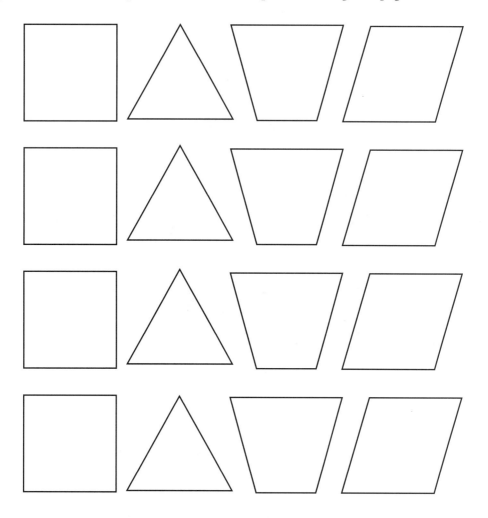

Sample Questions

You can find the answers to this section on page 92.

1. Francis Frog can jump 3 feet in one hop. How many feet can he jump in 9 hops?

   Show your work.

   Answer:_____

2. Amanda needs to practice her viola for a total of 60 minutes this school week. She practiced for 14 minutes on Monday, 20 minutes on Tuesday, 6 minutes on Wednesday, and 10 minutes on Thursday. How many minutes does she need to practice on Friday?

   Show your work.

   Answer:_____

3. Julian is planning a birthday party with his 5 friends, so there will be 6 people at the party altogether. If Julian orders 3 pizzas, each having 8 slices, how many slices of pizza will each person at the party get?

   Show your work.

   Answer:_____

4. At Mangino's Pizzeria, you get to create your own pizza. You can choose to have a regular pie or a Sicilian pie. For a topping you can chose mushrooms, peppers, or meatballs. And for your spice you can pick either garlic powder or oregano. How many possible pizza combinations could you make?

Show your work.

Answer:_____

5. Jack's mom had to go to the Discount Sporting Goods Store to buy some equipment. She wants to buy 5 baseballs for $1 each, 6 footballs for $3 each, and 3 soccer balls for $5 each. How much will she spend at the store?

Answer:_____

6. Jessica bought 3 boxes of oatmeal raisin cookies, 6 boxes of chocolate mint cookies, and 4 boxes of pecan cookies. Each box contains 8 cookies. How many cookies did Jessica buy altogether?

Answer:_____

7.

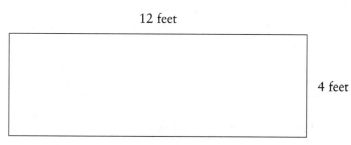

12 feet

4 feet

Part A: What is the perimeter of the rectangle?

Part B: What is the area of the rectangle?

8. Use your ruler to help you solve this problem.

Part A: Measure each piece of wood shown below to the nearest centimeter. Write the length in the space next to each picture.

_____ centimeters

_____ centimeters

_____ centimeters

_____ centimeters

_____ centimeters

Part B: Your art teacher wants you to keep only the pieces of wood that are shorter than centimeters. Circle each piece of wood that is *shorter* than 5 centimeters.

9. You may use your counters to help you solve this problem.

The recipe below shows how much of each item is needed to make one batch of Oatmeal Raisin Cookies.

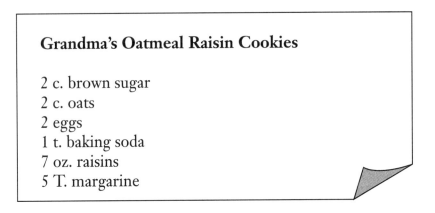

Grandma's Oatmeal Raisin Cookies

2 c. brown sugar
2 c. oats
2 eggs
1 t. baking soda
7 oz. raisins
5 T. margarine

For the school bake sale, you have to make 3 batches of Oatmeal Raisin Cookies. Complete the list below to show how much of each item will be needed.

_____c. brown sugar
_____c. oats
_____eggs
_____t. baking soda
_____oz. raisins
_____T. margarine

10. In the classroom, there are 3 square tables. There are 4 children sitting at each table. Each child has 3 crayons.

In the space below, draw a diagram or model to represent this information.

Find the total number of crayons.

Answer:_____crayons

11. Explain what a *quadrilateral* shape is:

_____

_____

In the space below, trace over one of your pattern blocks that is NOT a quadrilateral.

12. There are seven children standing in a row, in this order:

Alexandra - Jim - Zoey - Jacqueline - Brian - Jan - Xena

One child will be chosen to lead the parade. Use the clues to find out which child was chosen.

Clues:
1—The child's name has more than three letters but less than six.
2—The child is next to Jacqueline, but not next to Jan.

Which child was chosen?

Answer:_____

Explain the steps you used to find your answer.

_____

_____

_____

_____

_____

_____

_____

13. Randy has a bag of these colored plastic eggs. If Ralph reaches in without looking and grabs one, which two colors have an equal chance of being chosen?

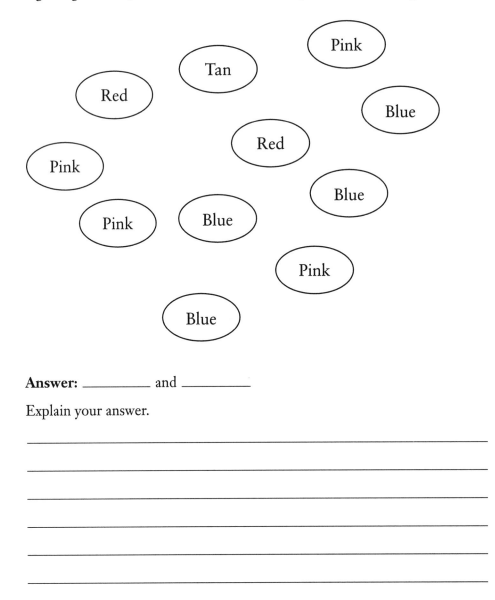

Answer: _____ and _____

Explain your answer.

_____

_____

_____

_____

_____

_____

14. The children at school were asked to name their favorite fast food. The results are shown in the table below.

Child	Favorite Food	Child	Favorite Food
Venessa	pizza	Joanna	pizza
Ryan	hot dog	Christina	pizza
Peter	hamburger	Jesse	hamburger
Nicholas	pizza	Dylan	hot dog
Amanda	hamburger	Michael	chicken nuggets
Rachel	chicken nuggets	Madison	chicken nuggets
Lenton	hot dog	Kevin	hamburger
Alija	chicken nuggets	Gina	pizza

On the grid below, make a bar graph showing the number of students who prefer each food. Use the information from the table to help you. *Remember to skip columns in your bar graph; otherwise it is a histogram!*
Be sure to:

▶ title the graph
▶ label the axes
▶ graph all the data

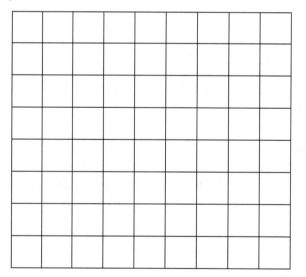

Using the information from your graph, write one statement comparing the food choices.

_____

_____

15. You may use your counters on page xvii to help you solve this problem. Below are some clues about the number of students in Mrs. Geiss's class.

▶ There are 4 more boys than girls in the class.
▶ There are a total of 20 kids in the class.

How many boys are in the class?

Answer:_____

On the lines below, explain how you found your answer.

_____

_____

_____

_____

_____

16. Johnny drove his truck for three days to get to the Colebrook House Hotel. When he left home, this was the total number of miles the truck had been driven:

9436

When he arrived at the Colebrook House, this was the total number of miles the truck had been driven:

10274

If Johnny drove 387 miles the first day, and 155 miles the second day, how many miles did he drive the third day?

Show your work.

Answer:_____

17. Mrs. Wild and her three children are going to the movies.

Movie Tickets:

Adults: $7.50

Children under 12: $4.25

How much will Mrs. Wild have to pay for herself and her three children—who are under 12—to go to the movies?

Show your work.

Answer: _____

18. Mr. Olszower is doing his laundry at the Discount Laundromat. The sign below shows how much it costs to wash and dry your laundry there.

Discount Laundromat

Washing Machines $1.00 per load

Dryers $0.75 per load

Mr. Olszower needs to wash and dry 3 loads of laundry. The machines only take quarters. Find how many quarters he will need to do his laundry.

Show your work.

Answer:_____

19. The chart below was hanging inside Mrs. Necroto's classroom.

DAY	ATTENDANCE
Monday	* * * * * * * *
Tuesday	* * * * * * *
Wednesday	* * * * * * * * *
Thursday	* * * * * *

Key: Each * represents 2 students present.

Part A: How many students were present in Mrs. Necroto's class on Wednesday?
Show your work.

Answer:_____

Part B: How many more students were present on Monday than on Thursday in Mrs. Necroto's class?

Answer:_____

Part C: There were 18 students in Mrs. Necroto's class on Friday. Complete the chart below by drawing in the correct number of *'s for Friday.

DAY	ATTENDANCE
Friday	

Key: Each * represents 2 students present.

On the lines below, explain the mathematics you used to find the number of *'s for Friday.

_____

_____

_____

20. Jim will spin the spinner.

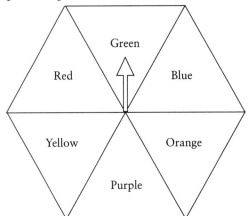

What is the probability the arrow will land on purple?

Answer:_____

On the lines below, explain in words how you found your answer.

_____

_____

_____

21.

NICOLE'S PLANT	
DAY	**HEIGHT IN MILLIMETERS**
1	4
2	8
3	12
4	16
5	20
6	?

If Nicole's plant continues to grow in the same pattern, how many millimeters tall will it be on day 6?

Answer:_____ millimeters

On the lines below, explain in words how you found your answer.

_____

_____

_____

22. On a car trip to the grocery store, Ellen, Deanna, and James looked out the car window and watched all the cars passing by. Ellen saw 12 red cars, Deanna saw 7 and James saw 10. Deanna wondered in what order should she add up the numbers to get the highest total. Does the order matter? On the lines below, explain why or why not.

_____

_____

_____

23. Lisa used pattern blocks to draw half of a design. Complete the design below so that the line is a line of symmetry. Trace around your pattern blocks to show the other half of the design.

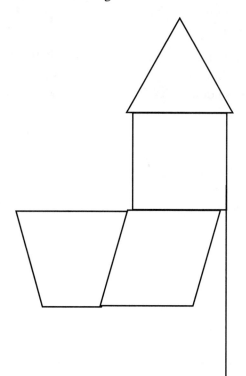

Practice Math Test

THIS PRACTICE test is similar to the ones you may take in your 4th grade class. The multiple-choice questions should take between 30–35 minutes. The open-ended questions can be done in two blocks of nine questions each, and should take approximately 45 minutes to one hour each. If it takes you longer than this to complete the test, remember that this is only a practice test. You may want to take it a second time to refine your skills. You can find the answers to this section on page 98.

1. Chris collects movies. He has 33 classic movies, 67 musicals, 48 comedies, and 21 science fiction. What is the best estimate of the total number of movies he has?
   a. between 50 and 100
   b. between 100 and 150
   c. between 150 and 200
   d. between 200 and 250

2. At the Pearsall Book Store, paperback books cost $6.99, hardcover books cost $21.49 and children's books cost $3.00. If Liz buys one paperback, one hardcover and 2 children's books, what is the total cost?
   a. $35.48
   b. $34.38
   c. $34.48
   d. $24.48

3. What is $\frac{1}{8} + \frac{4}{8}$?
   a. $\frac{1}{8}$
   b. $\frac{4}{8}$
   c. $\frac{5}{16}$
   d. $\frac{5}{8}$

4. Look at the pattern below:

   4, _____, 12, 16, 20, _____, 28, 23

   What are the two missing numbers?
   a. 6 and 24
   b. 8 and 26
   c. 8 and 24
   d. 9 and 24

5. Samantha started her homework at 4:00. She finished at 6:15. How many hours did she work?
   a. 2 hours and 15 minutes
   b. $2\frac{1}{2}$ hours
   c. 2 hours and 45 minutes
   d. 1 hour and 45 minutes

6. Tara decided to take a long boat trip down the coast. The first day she traveled 432 miles, the second day 267, the third day 198, and the fourth day 381. How many miles did she travel altogether?
   a. 1,268
   b. 1,278
   c. about 1,200
   d. 1,178

7. Clifford had 363 marbles. He lost 98 of them. How many does he have left?
   a. 265
   b. 461
   c. 255
   d. 98

8. Natalie is filling holiday bags for her 8 friends. She wants each friend to get 2 little toys and 4 chocolate candies. How many little toys and chocolate candies must she buy?
   a. 18 little toys and 24 chocolate candies
   b. 16 little toys and 32 chocolate candies
   c. 16 little toys and 24 chocolate candies
   d. 12 little toys and 24 chocolate candies

9. If Christine had a chocolate cake cut into 12 slices, and she invited 3 friends over to share it with her, how many slices would each person get?
   a. 2
   b. 4
   c. 3
   d. 6

10. Mrs. Rudolf needs 122 nails for her project. If the hardware store only sells nails in packages of 40, how many packages does she need to buy?
    a. 3
    b. 4
    c. 122
    d. 160

11. Tracy has $452.78 in her checking account. What is that amount rounded to the nearest dollar?
    a. $450
    b. $452
    c. $453
    d. $460

12. One side of this square is 7 feet. What is the area?

7 feet

    a. 14 ft.^{2}
    b. 17 ft.^{2}
    c. 28 ft.^{2}
    d. 49 ft.^{2}

13. What is the place value of 9 in the number 981, 203.7?
    a. tens
    b. hundred thousands
    c. thousands
    d. hundreds

14. Which number should be placed in the box below to make the equation true?
    72 – ☐ = 35
    a. 37
    b. 35
    c. 47
    d. 72

15. Which unit would most likely be used when measuring the weight of a nine-year-old girl?
    a. inches
    b. gallons
    c. ounces
    d. pounds

16. Each student in Mr. Gamberg's shop class will make a project using 12 blocks. What else do you need to know to find out how many blocks there are in all?
    a. the number of students in the class
    b. the type of project
    c. the number of blocks in a bag
    d. the size of the blocks

17. Patty exercised 18 hours each week for 8 weeks. Which sentence could be used to find the total number of hours she exercised?
    a. $18 - 8 =$ (total # of hours)
    b. (total # of hours) $+ 8 = 18$
    c. $18 \times 8 =$ (total # of hours)
    d. $18 + 8 =$ (total # of hours)

18. $(4 \times 7) - (6 \div 3) =$
    a. 24
    b. 26
    c. 25
    d. $\frac{4}{3}$

19. Melissa has 30 pens in a drawer. There are 12 black pens, 5 blue pens, 6 red pens and 7 green pens. If she reaches into the drawer and takes one pen out, what color will it *most likely* be?
    a. blue
    b. red
    c. green
    d. black

20. What is 5.4×3.7?
    a. 9.1
    b. 15.28
    c. 19.98
    d. 15

21. The graphs below show the gas mileage and prices of 4 cars. Which car gets about 35 miles to the gallon and costs about $27,000?

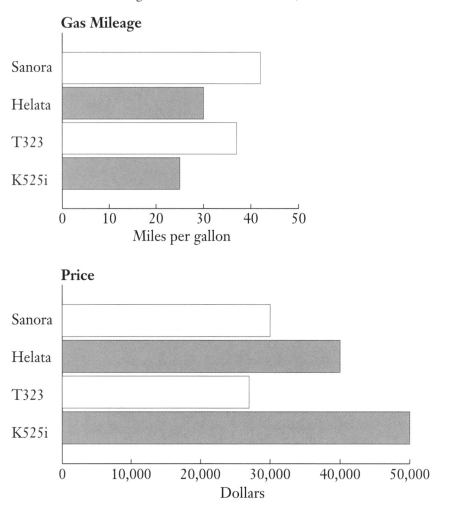

Gas Mileage

Price

a. Sanora
b. Helata
c. T323
d. K525i

22. Melanie has $5\frac{2}{3}$ yards of ribbon. She uses $3\frac{1}{3}$ yards to wrap presents. How many yards does she have left?

a. $2\frac{1}{3}$

b. $2\frac{2}{3}$

c. $1\frac{2}{3}$

d. $3\frac{1}{3}$

23. What is the perimeter of the rectangle below?

71

28

    a. 71
    b. 98
    c. 198
    d. 1,988

24. Which of the expressions below does not have the same value as the others?
    a. 16×3
    b. $4 \times 4 \times 2$
    c. 24×2
    d. $4 \times 2 \times 6$

25. Find the value of y if $y = 15 - x$, and $x = 5$.
    a. 5
    b. 15
    c. 20
    d. 10

Open-Ended Questions

1. Kaitlyn's Fern

WEEK	HEIGHT IN CENTIMETERS
1	6
2	12
3	18
4	24
5	30
6	36
7	?

If Kaitlyn's fern continues to grow in the same pattern, how many centimeters tall will it be in week 7?

Answer: _____ centimeters

On the lines below, explain in words how you found your answer.

_____

_____

_____

_____

_____

2. Amy will spin the spinner.

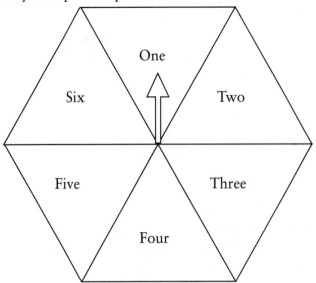

What is the probability the arrow will land on an even number?

Answer:_____

On the lines below, explain in words how you found your answer.

_____

_____

_____

_____

_____

3. Mrs. Gaston is taking her children on the rides at Play Land. The sign below shows how much it costs to go on the rides there.

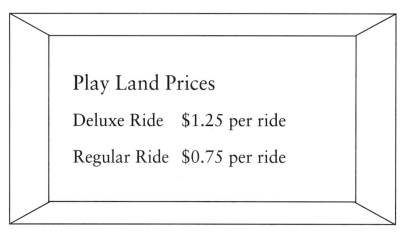

Play Land Prices

Deluxe Ride $1.25 per ride

Regular Ride $0.75 per ride

Mrs. Gaston is taking her children on 1 "Deluxe" ride and on 2 "Regular" rides. The machines only take quarters. Find how many quarters she will need to let her children go on their rides.

Show your work.

Answer: _____

4. Mr. Mona and his two children are going to the Ice Show.

Ice Show Tickets:

Adults: $21.50

Children under 12: $17.75

How much will Mr. Mona have to pay to take himself and his two children—who are under 12—to the Ice Show?

Show your work.

Answer: $_____

5. Mallory drove her motorcycle for three days to get to Virginia. When she left home, this was the total number of miles the motorcycle had been driven:

14,532

When she arrived in Virginia, this was the total number of miles the motorcycle had been driven:

18,123

If Mallory drove 1,221 miles the first day, and 1,354 miles the second day, how many miles did she drive the third day?

Show your work.

Answer:_____

6. You may use your counters on page xvii to help you solve this problem. Below are some facts about the number of pets in Pet Training School.

▶ There are 6 more cats than dogs in the class.
▶ There is a total of 24 pets in the class.

How many dogs are in the class?

Answer:_____
On the lines below, explain how you found your answer.

_____

_____

_____

7. The children at school were asked to choose their favorite color. The results are shown in the table below.

Child	Favorite Color	Child	Favorite Color
Victor	pink	John	green
Rob	blue	Charles	blue
Paul	green	Justin	purple
Nancy	pink	Debbie	pink
Allison	purple	Michele	purple
Ricky	blue	Marilyn	blue
Lucy	purple	Kathy	purple
Albert	green		

On the grid below, make a bar graph showing the number of students who prefer each color. Use the information from the table to help you. Be sure to:

▶ title the graph
▶ label the axes
▶ graph all the data

Using the information from your graph, write one statement comparing the color choices.

_____

_____

8. Kayla has a box of colored marbles. If Sheron reaches in without looking and grabs one, which color has the greatest chance of being chosen?

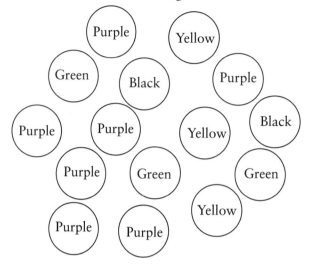

Answer:_____

Explain your answer.

_____

_____

_____

9. There are eight children standing in a row, in this order:

Michael - Nicholas - Lenny - Bridget - Mackenzie - Tom - Pete - Devon

One child will be chosen to be hall monitor. Use the clues to find out which child was chosen.

Clues:
1—The child's name has more than four letters but less than eight.
2—The child is next to Nicholas.
3—The child is not on the end.

Which child was chosen?

Answer:_____

Explain the steps you used to find your answer.

_____

_____

_____

10. In the Resource Room, there are 2 square tables. There are 8 children sitting at each table. Each child has 9 pencils.

Find the total number of pencils.

In the space below, draw a diagram or model to represent this information.

Answer: _____ pencils

11. You may use your counters on page xvii to help you solve this problem. The recipe below shows how much of each item is needed to make one batch of Peanut Butter Chip Cookies.

Peanut Butter Chip Cookies

1 c. sugar
$1\frac{1}{2}$ c. unbleached flour
3 egg whites
2 t. baking soda
12 oz. peanut butter chips
6 oz. chocolate chips
3 T. margarine or butter

For the Holiday Fair, you promised to make 4 batches of Peanut Butter Chip Cookies. Complete the list below to show how much of each item will be needed.

_____ c. sugar

_____ c. unbleached flour

_____ egg whites

_____ t. baking soda

_____ oz. peanut butter chips

_____ oz. chocolate chips

_____ T. margarine or butter

12. Use your ruler to help you solve this problem.

   Part A: Measure each piece of block shown below to the nearest centimeter. Write the length in the space next to each picture.

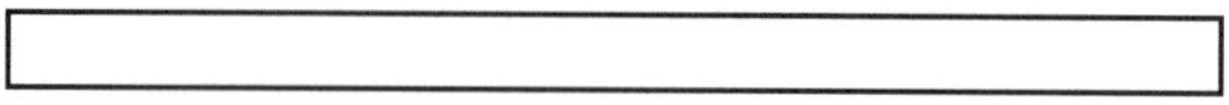

   _____ centimeters

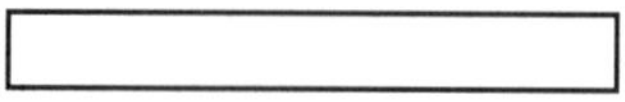

   _____ centimeters

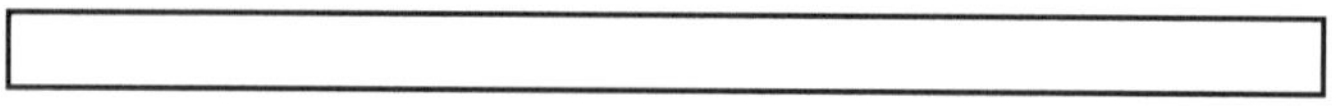

   _____ centimeters

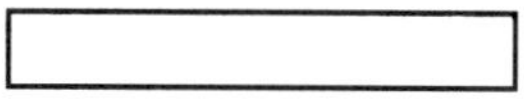

   _____ centimeters

   _____ centimeters

   Part B: Your shop teacher wants you to keep only the blocks that are longer than 7 centimeters. Circle each block that is _longer_ than 7 centimeters.

13.

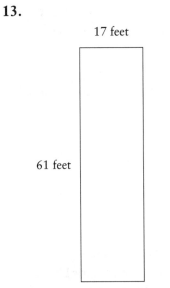

17 feet

61 feet

Part A: What is the perimeter of the rectangle?

Answer:_____

Show your work.

Part B: What is the area of the rectangle?

Answer:_____

Show your work.

14. Laurie bought 2 boxes of peanut butter cups, 7 boxes of chocolate mints and 6 boxes of pecan turtle candies. Each box contains 12 candies. How many candies did Laurie buy altogether?

    Answer:_____

15. Teresa had to go to the clothing store to buy some clothes. She wants to buy 4 shirts for $15 each, 5 pairs of pants for $30 each, and 2 dresses for $20 each. How much will she spend at the store?

    Answer:_____

16. Anthony is planning a party with his 11 friends, so there will be a total of 12 people at the party. If Anthony orders 6 pies, each having 8 slices, how many slices of pie will each person at the party get?

    Show your work.

    Answer:_____

17. Raymond needs to practice baseball for a total of 3 hours this school week. He practiced for 30 minutes on Monday, 23 minutes on Tuesday, 61 minutes on Wednesday, and 42 minutes on Thursday. How many minutes does he need to practice on Friday?

Show your work.

Answer: _____

18. Bobbie Bunny can jump 4 feet in one hop. How many feet can she jump in 7 hops?

Show your work.

Answer: _____

Answers to Sample Questions

1. You can draw a picture, chart, or graph if you need to.
   H = 1 foot   HHH = 1 hop

1 hop	2 hops	3 hops
HHH	HHH	HHH
3	6	9

4 hops	5 hops	6 hops
HHH	HHH	HHH
12	15	18

7 hops	8 hops	9 hops
HHH	HHH	HHH
21	24	27

   $3 \times 9 = 27$ feet.

   Francis Frog can hop 27 feet in 9 hops.

   You can explain how you arrived at your answer if you want:

   I multiplied 3×9; the 3 came from 3 feet in one hop and the 9 came from how many hops he took. It equaled 27, so 27 feet in 9 hops is the answer.

2. Again, you can draw a chart if you need to.
   One slash equals one minute of practice.

Mon.	Tues .	Wed.	Thurs.
/////	/////	/////	/////
/////	/////	/	/////
////	/////		
	/////		

   14 + 20 + 6 + 10 = 50

   Write a number sentence:

   $14 + 20 + 6 + 10 = 50$
   $60 - 50 = 10$ more minutes needed.

   Amanda needs to practice 10 more minutes on Friday.

3. You can draw or write a number sentence to show your work.

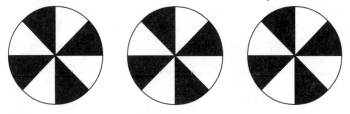

8 slices + 8 slices + 8 slices = 24 slices or
$3 \times 8 = 24$
$24 \div 6 = 4$ slices for each person.

Each person will get 4 slices of pizza.

4.

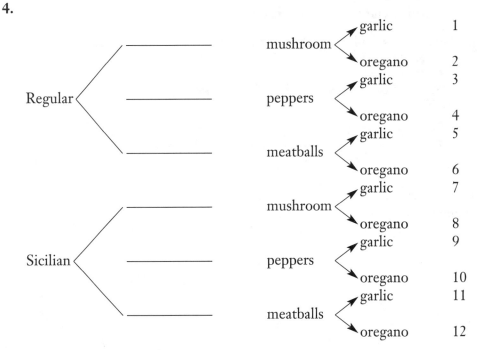

$2 + 2 + 2 = 6$ choices for regular and $2 + 2 + 2 = 6$ choices for Sicilian.
$6 + 6 = 12$ choices total.

At Mangino's Pizzeria you can make 12 different pizzas.

5. You can show your work.

B = Baseball,	F = Football,	S = Soccer Ball
B = $1	F = $3	S = $5
B = $1	F = $3	S = $5
B = $1	F = $3	S = $5
B = $1	F = $3	
B = $1	F = $3	
	F = $3	
Total = $5	Total = $18	Total = $15
$(5 \times 1 = 5)$	$(6 \times 3 = 18)$	$(3 \times 5 = 15)$

Now, I will add them together:

$5 + $18 + $15 = $38

She will spend $38 at the store.

6. You can draw a picture or make marks if you want, but it is not necessary.
   o = 1 cookie

Box 1 of O.R.	Box 1 of C.M.	Box 1 of P.
oooo	oooo	oooo
oooo	oooo	oooo
Box 2 of O.R.	Box 2 of C.M.	Box 2 of P.
oooo	oooo	oooo
oooo	oooo	oooo
Box 3 of O.R.	Box 3 of C.M.	Box 3 of P.
oooo	oooo	oooo
oooo	oooo	oooo
	Box 4 of C.M	Box 4 of P.
	oooo	oooo
	oooo	oooo
	Box 5 of C.M.	
	oooo	
	oooo	
	Box 6 of C.M.	
	oooo	
	oooo	
Total O.R.=	Total C.M.=	Total P.=
$3 \times 8 = 24$	$6 \times 8 = 48$	$4 \times 8 = 32$

$24 + 48 + 32 = 104$ cookies altogether.

Jessica bought 104 cookies.

7. **Part A:**
   $12 + 4 + 12 + 4 = 32$

   The perimeter of the rectangle is 32 feet.

   Part B:
   $12 \times 4 = 48$

   The area is 48 square feet.

8. **Part A:** From top to bottom, the measurements of the wood are 7 cm, 3.5 cm, 9 cm, 1.5 cm, and 5.5 cm.

   Part B: Only the second and fourth pieces of wood should be circled.

9. You need to multiply all the ingredients by 3, so it will be **6 c. brown sugar, 9 c. oats, 6 eggs, 3 t. baking soda, 21 oz. raisins, 15 T. margarine.**

10.

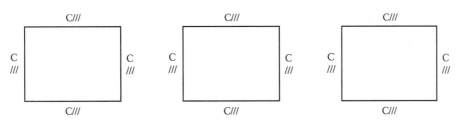

   $3 \times 4 \times 3 = \textbf{36 crayons}$

11. **A quadrilateral is a shape that has four sides.** The children can trace their triangle pattern block.

12. **Zoey is the child who was chosen.**
    Steps:
    The child's name has more than three letters but less than six, so it can't be Alexandra, Jim, Jacqueline, or Jan.
    It can't be Brian and Xena because they are next to Jan, so that leaves Zoey.

13. **Pink and blue have an equal chance of being chosen.**

    Pink has a $\frac{4}{11}$ chance of being chosen. Blue also has a $\frac{4}{11}$ chance of being chosen. Red has a $\frac{2}{11}$ chance of being chosen and tan has a $\frac{1}{11}$ chance of being chosen.

14. This is what your graph could look like:

Favorite Fast Foods

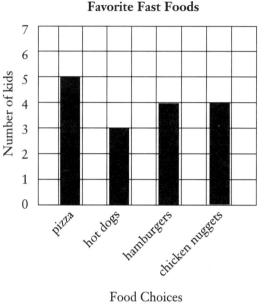

Food Choices

Write one fact. It could be any one of the following:

The same number of children like hamburgers and chicken nuggets.
More kids like pizza than any other food.
Hot dogs were the least popular in the class.
One more person liked pizza than hamburgers.

15. There are 12 boys in the class.
One way to figure this out is to say that there are ☐ girls in the class and since there are 4 more boys than girls, or "plus four" boys, you can say that there are ☐ + 4 boys in the class. Since there are 20 kids altogether, you can make a number sentence like this:

☐ + ☐ + 4 = 20
(girls) (boys) = Total in class

Then you can subtract four from both sides to get:

☐ + ☐ = 16

Then ask yourself, "what plus what equals 16?" The answer is 8. Then you know there are 8 girls in the class and 8 + 4 boys in the class, which equals 12.

You can check your work. Is the number of boys four more than the number of girls? Yes, because 12 − 8 = 4.

And is the total equal to twenty? Yes, because 12 + 8 = 20.

Another, easier way to figure this out may be just to use your counters on page xvii and test a bunch of numbers until you get the right combination.

16. This question has multiple steps, but it is relatively easy if you are careful. First you have to figure out how many miles Johnny drove in total, which is $10274 - 9436 = 838$. Then you can simply add up the miles he drove the first and second day ($387 + 155 = 542$) and then subtract that number from the original total: $838 - 542 = 296$ miles.

   He drove 296 miles the third day.

17. Mrs. Wild will have to pay $7.50 for herself, plus $4.25 + $4.25 + $4.25 for her children. $7.50 + $4.25 + $4.25 + $4.25 = $20.25.

   The answer is $20.25.

18. First you can see how much it would cost to do 3 loads of wash:

   $3 \times 1.00 = 3.00$.

   Then you can calculate how much it would cost to dry 3 loads: $3 \times 0.75 = 2.25$.
   Then add them together: $3.00 + 2.25 = 5.25$
   But you are not done yet; remember, the question is asking you how many *quarters* you need, not how much money. To find this you must know that *there are 4 quarters in $1.00*, so multiply by five to find out how many are in $5.00: $4 \times 5 = 20$. There are 20 quarters in $5.00. Add on one extra quarter, since the total is $5.25, and your final answer is 21.

   He will need 21 quarters.

19. **Part A:**
   Each $\times$ = 2 students, and there were 8 $\times$'s, so $2 \times 8 = 16$.

   The answer is 16 students.

   Part B:
   Remember that each ∗ = 2 students, so to find out how many were there on Monday, 8 stars × 2 = 16 children. On Thursday there were $6 \times 2 = 12$ children. $16 - 12 = 4$. If you put 2 as your answer then you just subtracted stars, not the students they represented.

   The answer is 4 students.

   Part C:

Day	Attendance
Friday	∗ ∗ ∗ ∗ ∗ ∗ ∗ ∗ ∗

   There are 9 stars. I knew that there were 18 students, and since each star is equal to 2 students, I divided 18 by 2 to get 9 stars. I know this is right because $2 \times 9 = 18$ students.

20. **The probability that the arrow will land on purple is $\frac{1}{6}$.** This is because there are 6 color choices and purple is one out of those six.

21. **24 millimeters**. I know this because the pattern was going up by 4 each time, so I added 4 to 20 to get 24.

22. With addition, it doesn't matter in which order you add the numbers. 12 + 7 + 10 = 29 and 7 + 10 + 12 = 29 and 10 + 12 + 7 = 29, etc.

23. Your design should be a mirror image of the one Lisa created.

Practice Math Test Answers

1. **c.** If you add up all the movies Chris has, you will see that it comes to 169 total, which is between 150 and 200.

2. **c.** Simply line up your decimal points and add them up. 6.99 + 21.49 + 3.00 + 3.00 = 34.48.

3. **d.** $\frac{1}{8} + \frac{4}{8} = \frac{5}{8}$. The denominator (bottom number) stays the same.

4. **c.** This pattern is counting by fours, so the missing numbers are 8 and 24.

5. **a.** If Samantha started at 4:00 and ended at 6:15, she worked for 2 hours and 15 minutes.

6. **b.** Add up all the miles Tara traveled: 432 + 267 + 198 + 381 = 1,278.

7. **a.** Subtract: 363 − 98 = 265.

8. **b.** $2 \times 8 = 16$ little toys and $4 \times 8 = 32$ chocolate candies.

9. **c.** This is a division problem. $12 \div 4 = 3$ slices each. If you picked answer **b** then you probably forgot to count Christine.

10. **b.** She needs 122 nails. If the hardware store only sells them in packages of 40, you need to find out how many packages she needs. 3 packs × 40 nails = 120 nails which is not enough, but 4 packs × 40 nails = 160. If you chose answer **d** you chose the number of nails she would be buying, not the number of packages.

11. **c.** $452.78 rounded to the nearest dollar is $453. If you picked answer **a** you rounded to the nearest ten, and if you picked answer **b** you rounded down, not up, which is nearer.

12. **d.** Area = length × width. A square's four sides are all the same, so Area = 7 × 7, which is 49. If you picked answer **c** you were probably thinking of the perimeter. The perimeter is when you add all the sides together.

13. **b.** The 9 is in the hundred thousands place.

14. **a.** When you see this question, think to yourself, "72 minus what equals 35?" 72 − 37 = 35. You can find this answer by figuring out that 72 − 35 = 37.

15. **d.** You would use inches to measure the length of something, not the weight, so it isn't answer **a**. Gallons are used to measure liquids, so it is not answer **b**. And ounces are used to measure something under a pound—there are 16 ounces in a pound—so it is not answer **c**. You can also think of what happens when you are weighed—they tell you how many pounds you weigh.

16. **a.** To find out how many blocks there are in all, you need to find out how many students there are in the class. You can then multiply that number by 12 to find out how many blocks there are in all. If you look at the other answers, you will notice that it doesn't matter what type of project it is, the number of blocks in a bag, or the size of the blocks.

17. **c.** If you want to find the total number of hours Patty exercised, you would multiply 18×8 to get your answer.

18. **b.** Do what is in the parentheses first: $4 \times 7 = 28$ and $6 \div 3 = 2$. Then figure out $28 - 2 = 26$.

19. **d.** The chance of picking a black pen is $\frac{12}{30}$. The chance of picking a blue pen is $\frac{5}{30}$, a red pen is $\frac{6}{30}$ and a green pen is $\frac{7}{30}$. Since you have the greatest chance of picking a black pen, that is the color it will most likely be.

20. **c.** $5.4 \times 3.7 = 19.98$.

21. **c.** To answer this question, you need to read the chart. The answer is not answer **a** because the Sanora gets about 40 miles to the gallon and costs about $30,000. It is not answer **b** because the Helata gets about 30 miles per gallon and costs about $42,000. And it is not answer **d** because the K525i gets about 25 miles per gallon and costs about $50,000. The correct answer is **c** because the T323 gets about 35 miles per gallon and costs about $27,000.

22. **a.** $\frac{52}{3} - 3\frac{1}{3} = \frac{21}{3}$.

23. **c.** To find the perimeter you have to add all the sides: $71 + 71 + 28 + 28 = 198$. If you picked answer **d** you found the area.

24. **b.** The easiest way to figure this out is to solve all the problems. $16 \times 3 = 48$, $4 \times 4 \times 2 = 32$, $24 \times 2 = 48$, $4 \times 2 \times 6 = 48$, so the answer is **b** because it does not have the same value.

25. **d.** If $y = 15 - x$, you simply replace x with the value they give you, which is 5, and then it looks like $y = 15 - 5$, which is 10.

Open-Ended Questions

1. **42 centimeters.** I know this because the pattern was going up by 6 each time, so I added 6 to 36 to get 42.

2. **The probability that the arrow will land on an even number is $\frac{3}{6}$.** This is because there are 6 number choices and there are three even numbers out of those six.

3. First you can see how much it would cost to go on the rides. One "Deluxe" ride will cost $1.25, plus 2 "Regular" rides which cost $0.75 + $0.75 = $1.50. Add them together to get $1.25 + $1.50 = $2.75.

   But you are not done yet; remember, the question is asking you how many *quarters* you need, not how much money. To find this you must know that there are 4 quarters in $1.00, so multiply 4×2 (as in the 2 dollars) to get 8 quarters. Then 75 cents is another 3 quarters, for a total of 11 quarters.

She will need 11 quarters.

4. Mr. Mona will have to pay $21.50 for himself, plus $17.75 + $17.75 for his children. $21.50 + $17.75 + $17.75 = **$57.00.**

5. This question has multiple steps, but it is relatively easy if you are careful. First you have to figure out how many miles Mallory drove in total, which is $18,123 - 14,532 = 3,591$. Then you can simply add up the miles she drove the first and second day ($1,221 + 1,354 = 2,575$) and then subtract that number from the original total: $3,591 - 2,575 = 1,016$ miles. **She drove 1,016 miles the third day.**

6. **There are 9 dogs in the class.**

   One way to figure this out is to say that there are ☐ dogs in the class and since there are 6 more cats than dogs, or "plus six" cats, you can say that there are ☐ + 6 cats in the class. Since there are 24 pets altogether, you can make a number sentence like this:

   ☐ + ☐ + 6 = 24
   (dogs) (cats) = Total in class

   Then you can minus six from both sides to get:

   ☐ + ☐ = 18

   Then ask yourself "what plus what equals 18?" The answer is 9. Then you know there are 9 dogs in the class and 9 + 5 cats in the class, which equals 15.

   You can check your work. Is the number of cats six more than the number of dogs? Yes, because $15 - 9 = 6$.

   And is the total equal to twenty-four? Yes, because $15 + 9 = 24$.

   Another way to figure this out may be just to use your counters on page xvii and test a bunch of numbers until you get the right combination.

7. This is what your graph could look like:
(Remember to skip columns in your bar graph; otherwise it is a histogram!

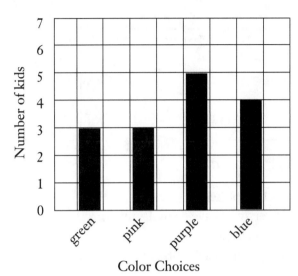

Write one fact. It could be any one of the following:

The same number of children like pink and green.
More kids like purple than any other color.
One more person liked purple than blue.

8. **Purple has the greatest chance of being chosen.** Purple has a $\frac{7}{15}$ chance of being chosen. Yellow has a $\frac{3}{15}$ chance of being chosen, green has a $\frac{3}{15}$ chance of being chosen, and black has a $\frac{2}{15}$ chance.

9. **Lenny is the child who was chosen.**
Steps:

The child's name has more than 4 letters but less than 8, so it can't be Nicholas, Mackenzie, Tom, or Pete.

The child is next to Nicholas, so it has to be Lenny or Michael.

The child is not on the end, so it has to be Lenny.

10.

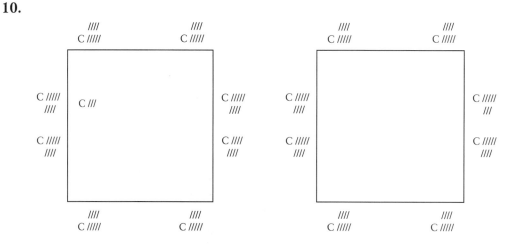

$2 \times 8 \times 9 = $ **144 pencils.**

11. For the answers you have to multiply everything by 4.

__**4**__ c. sugar

__1.5 × 4 = 6__ c. unbleached flour

__**12**__ egg whites

__**8**__ t. baking soda

__**48**__ oz. peanut butter chips

__**24**__ oz. chocolate chips

__**12**__ T. margarine or butter

12. **Part A:** From top to bottom, the measurements of the blocks are 8.3 cm, 4.2 cm, 9 cm, 3.5 cm, 6.7 cm.

Part B: The only two blocks longer than 7 cm are the first and third blocks.

13. **Part A:** 17 + 17 + 61 + 61 = 156

The perimeter of the rectangle 156 is feet.

Part B: $17 \times 61 = 1037$

The area is 1,037 square feet.

14. You can draw a picture or make marks if you want, but it is not necessary. But remember to show your work!

First I multiplied to find out how many candies of each kind there were:

Total Peanut Butter =   Total Mint =   Total Pecan =
$2 \times 12 = 24$ $7 \times 12 = 84$ $6 \times 12 = 72$

Then, I added them together to get the total:
24 + 84 + 72 = 180.

Laurie bought 180 candies altogether.

Another way you can say it is:

First I added the number of boxes she bought altogether:
2 + 7 + 6 = 15

Then I multiplied that by the number of candies in each box:
15 × 12 = 180

Laurie bought 180 candies altogether.

15. You can show your work

S = Shirt	P = Pants	D = Dress
S = $15	P = $30	D = $20
S = $15	P = $30	D = $20
S = $15	P = $30	
S = $15	P = $30	
	P = $30	

Total = $60   Total = $150   Total = $40
(4 × 15 = 60)   (5 × 30 = 150)   (2 × 20 = 40)

Now, I will add them together:
$60 + $150 + $40 = $250

She will spend $250 at the store.

16.

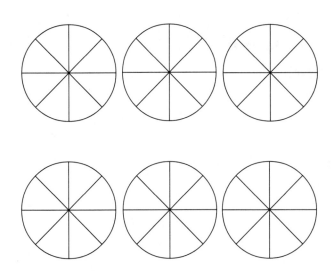

8 + 8 + 8 + 8 + 8 + 8 = 48 or
6 pies × 8 slices = 48 slices total

Next, I divide by the number of people there:
48 ÷ 12 = 4 slices for each person.

Each person will get 4 slices of pie.

17.   First I added up all the minutes he practiced:
30 + 23 + 61 + 42 = 156

Then I subtracted the amount he practiced from the total amount he needs to practice:
180 − 156 = 24 more minutes needed. (Remember there are 180 minutes in 3 hours. There are 60 minutes in 1 hour, so 60 × 3 = 180)

Raymond needs to practice 24 more minutes on Friday.

18.   You can draw a picture if you need to.
H = 1 foot   HHHH = 1 hop

1 hop	2 hops	3 hops
HHHH	HHHH	HHHH
4	8	12

4 hops	5 hops	6 hops
HHHH	HHHH	HHHH
16	20	24

7 hops
HHHH
28

4 feet × 7 hops = 28 feet

Bobbie Bunny can hop 28 feet in 7 hops.

CHAPTER

English/Language Arts Practice

The English section of the 4th grade assessment tests will include reading comprehension passages with multiple-choice questions. While reading, children are permitted to refer back to the passages any time they need to during the test. In other words, the answers are right there in the text, so they should go back and look! Make sure they know NOT to try to answer all the questions from memory. The questions can be tricky, and the students are given ample time for this section, so it would be foolish to rush through and not go back to the story.

Sometimes, however, a question will ask for the meaning of a particular word in a certain sentence. It is up to the student to go back to the passage and figure out the correct meaning. If your child does not know the meaning of the word, tell him to try to pick what makes the most sense in the context of that sentence. Then tell him to eliminate all obviously wrong answers, and take his best guess. With multiple-choice questions there is still a good chance of getting a question right even if you don't know the answer.

In the multiple-choice section, students are being tested on the ability to read and understand the printed word. This is where the children have to uncover facts and ideas, find relationships, make generalizations, and interpret information. Literary response, critical analysis, and evaluation of the text will be discussed in the next chapter.

Practice with these simple passages to help your child understand literal level questions that require knowledge of facts and details.

Passage One

Christopher Columbus

Christopher Columbus was born in Genoa, Italy in 1451. He liked to look out over the water from the window of his house. He dreamed of one day becoming a sailor. For a while he lived in Portugal with his brother. While in Portugal, Columbus married and had a son.

Christopher Columbus always heard people talking about sailing east. They would have to sail around Africa to get to the Indies. The Indies were India, China, and Japan. People purchased valuable jewels, cloth, clothes, animals, spices, and other exotic things there.

Columbus knew that the earth was round, and thought that he could get to the Indies more quickly if he sailed west. He asked King John II of Portugal for ships so he could try, but the king refused. The kings of France and England refused as well.

Christopher went to King Ferdinand and Queen Isabella of Spain to ask for ships. They gave him three ships. The ships were the Niña, the Pinta, and the Santa Maria. The year was 1492, and Christopher Columbus had many eager men to sail with him.

On October 12, 1492, the men aboard ship spotted land. It was an island southwest of Florida. Christopher and some men rowed ashore. Christopher put a flag in the ground and claimed the island for Spain.

Columbus believed he reached the Indies. He didn't realize he had reached America. He called the native peoples of the island "Indians." He gave them glass bead necklaces and hats to wear.

In 1493, Columbus went back to Spain. He brought with him a little bit of gold, some parrots, and a couple of Indians. Some sailors stayed behind to look for more gold.

Columbus became a hero. The king and queen honored him, as did the people of Spain. Columbus made four voyages to America in all. He died in 1506 in Spain.

1. Where was Columbus born?
   a. Italy
   b. Portugal
   c. Spain
   d. France

2. What did Columbus dream of becoming?
   a. a king
   b. wealthy
   c. a sailor
   d. a trader

3. In what direction did sailors usually go to get to the Indies?
   a. north
   b. south
   c. east
   d. west

4. What were the Indies?
   a. jewels and spices
   b. Indiana
   c. Africa, China, Japan, and India
   d. India, China, and Japan.

5. What did people buy in the Indies?
   a. jewels
   b. clothes
   c. spices
   d. all of the above

6. In what year did he make his first voyage?
   a. 1451
   b. 1492
   c. 1493
   d. 1506

7. What did Columbus give to the Indians?
   a. glass bead necklaces
   b. lace handkerchiefs
   c. money
   d. gold

8. How many voyages did Columbus make to America?
   a. 1
   b. 2
   c. 3
   d. 4

Passage Two

Abraham Lincoln

Abraham **Lincoln** was born on February 12, 1809 in a little log cabin in Kentucky. He helped on his father's farm. He was very tall and thin, but a hard worker. When he wasn't working on the farm he would walk many miles to and from school. He would also walk long distances to borrow books. It didn't matter to him what the weather was like. He loved to read and learn. He would often read by candlelight late at night.

When Lincoln was seven, his family moved to Indiana. When he was nine years old, his mother died. When he was 21, his family moved to Illinois. The next year he went to New Orleans. While he was there he saw a slave market for the first time. This greatly affected him. He was very upset to see people being treated this way.

Lincoln began to study law when he was 25. He moved to Springfield, Illinois and became a lawyer at the age of 27. He ran for public office, and he was a member of the Illinois Legislature and later, a member of the House of Representatives. In 1858, he ran against Stephen Douglas to try to become a senator. They had many debates and Lincoln spoke out against slavery. Lincoln lost the election, but the debates made him famous. In 1860, he ran against Douglas again, only this time it was for the presidency. And this time, Lincoln won.

In the South at this time there were over three million slaves. The southern states did not want to give up having slaves, so they broke away from the United States. Eleven southern states formed the Confederate States of America.

In April of 1861 the war began between the North and the South. It was the first and only time our country had a Civil War. Abraham Lincoln was the leader in the North and Jefferson Davis was the leader of the South. General Ulysses S. Grant led the Northern armies and Robert E. Lee led the Southern armies. There was very fierce fighting, sometimes pitting brother against brother.

During that time Lincoln wrote the Emancipation Proclamation. The document stated that all the slaves were free. And in 1863, he gave the famous Gettysburg Address.

Lincoln was re-elected president in 1864, and in April of 1865 the war ended. The South surrendered to the North.

A few days after the war ended Lincoln went to see a play with his wife. During the play, a man named John Wilkes Booth shot the president, and Lincoln died the next day. Millions of Americans mourned the death of a great man. His nickname was "Honest Abe" and many people thought he was our greatest president.

QUESTIONS

1. Where was Abraham Lincoln born?
   a. Illinois
   b. Indiana
   c. Kentucky
   d. New Orleans

2. What did Abraham love to do?
   a. work on the farm
   b. walk to school in the bad weather
   c. read and learn
   d. ride a horse

3. What did Lincoln see for the first time in New Orleans?
   a. law books
   b. the Mississippi River
   c. a slave market
   d. none of the above

4. How did Lincoln feel when he first saw the slave market?
   a. excited
   b. he didn't really care
   c. he was very upset
   d. he was tired

5. What was the Emancipation Proclamation?
   a. The document that said all slaves were free.
   b. The document that said the war was over.
   c. The document that said the war had just begun.
   d. A new set of laws regarding the war.

6. Who led the Northern Armies during the war?
   a. Stephen Douglas
   b. Jefferson Davis
   c. Ulysses S. Grant
   d. Robert E. Lee

7. What was Lincoln's nickname?
   a. Dishonest Abe
   b. The father of our country
   c. The greatest president
   d. Honest Abe

8. How old was Lincoln when his mother died?
   a. seven
   b. nine
   c. twenty-one
   d. twenty-five

Passage Three

IN THIS AND the next several passages, your child may have to take some extra steps as he or she goes beyond the literal level to interpret and apply the knowledge he or she is gaining from the passage.

Billy's Bicycle

Billy opened his birthday present with excitement. He had a feeling it was the bike he had asked for. He tore open the paper and he was right! It was the blue one with the silver horn and the red reflectors in the back and the front. He was so excited he could hardly contain himself.

"Mom, Mom, can I go out and ride now?" Billy asked. "I just know I'll be able to do it!"

"Well, Billy," said his mother, "remember this is a two-wheel bike. It's going to take a lot of practice to learn how to ride it."

"Don't worry Mom! I'm sure I'll be able to learn how very quickly!"

"Okay. Put on your knee pads and your helmet and you can go outside. Just be careful."

"Thanks, Mom!" Billy shouted as he ran off down the hall to get ready. Once he was outside, he steadied his bike and balanced himself up on the seat. He pushed off with his feet, pedaled once, and then fell right over with a crash. He hurt his wrist and skinned his elbow. He went running into the house.

"Mom! I hurt myself!" he cried. Tears streamed down his face and he sniffled.

"Are you okay Billy?" his mom asked. "Let me see. Oh, that's only a little scrape. Let me clean it up." She took Billy into the bathroom and washed his elbow, then cleaned it with alcohol. Billy screamed and cried.

"I'm never going to ride that stupid bike again!" he shouted. "Never, never, never!"

"Now Billy," his mom said, kneeling down to look him in the eyes, "don't give up. Things that are worthwhile often don't come easy. Sometimes you have to try again and again and again before you can learn something new. Just don't give up."

Billy mumbled and walked away. He decided he still wasn't going to ride his bike. It was just too hard. He walked outside and sat on the porch steps. A few minutes later Billy's older brother Adam came over and sat down next to him.

"What's the matter?" Adam asked Billy.

"I can't ride my bike. It's too hard."

"This reminds me of last year, when I was trying to learn how to skateboard," said Adam. "Do you remember? I used to fall down and get bruised all the time. But I really wanted to learn, and I never gave up. And now look at what I can do!"

Billy smiled. His brother was a whiz on the skateboard. Adam talked Billy into trying again. He got up on the bike, pushed off and started to fall again. But this time he caught himself. He tried again and again. He was out there all day. He kept falling and he kept getting back on and trying again. His brother, mother, and father kept cheering him on.

Then, suddenly he figured out how to balance. He did it! He was riding his bike!

1. What sport was Adam trying to learn when he kept falling down?
   a. bike riding
   b. snowboarding
   c. skiing
   d. skateboarding

2. What is the best moral of this story?
   a. If at first you don't succeed, try and try again.
   b. Better late than never.
   c. Don't put off until tomorrow what you can do today.
   d. The early bird catches the worm.

3. What is the color of Billy's horn?
   a. gold
   b. silver
   c. blue
   d. red

4. In this story, what does the expression "he could hardly contain himself" mean?
   a. He couldn't fit himself into a container.
   b. He couldn't ride his bike.
   c. He couldn't hold in his excitement.
   d. He couldn't give up.

5. Who was cheering Billy on when he was trying to learn how to ride?
   a. his mother
   b. his father
   c. his brother
   d. all of the above

6. What does "skinned" mean?
   a. peeled the skin off
   b. got some extra skin on
   c. got a big bump
   d. washed

7. What did Billy need to learn how to do to ride?
   a. how to balance
   b. how to push off with his feet
   c. how to run
   d. how to keep his bike clean

8. What is Billy's father's name?
   a. Adam
   b. Billy Sr.
   c. Warren
   d. His name wasn't given.

Passage Four

Rocks

Rocks are made mostly from minerals. Rocks can be grouped into three different types: igneous, sedimentary, and metamorphic. Rocks are classified by composition and texture.

The surface of the earth is made of igneous rock. Igneous rocks are formed when magma cools. Magma is melted rock, like the stuff that flows out of a volcano. The word "igneous" means "fire rock." The rock deep inside our planet is heated by the great weight of all the rock above pressing down. The rock melts and becomes magma. Igneous rocks can be formed above or below the ground. Granite and basalt are examples of igneous rock.

Sedimentary rocks are formed from sediment. Sediment can be made up of pieces of sand, shell, mud, or organic material that has been transported from one place to another. Sediment can be moved by wind, water, ice, or gravity. When the movement stops, these pieces settle in layers. When these layers harden, sedimentary rock is formed. Shale and limestone are sedimentary rocks that are made underwater.

When igneous and sedimentary rocks are exposed to extreme heat and pressure, metamorphic rocks are created. For example, slate is made from shale, marble is made from limestone, and gneiss is a type of rock that is made from granite.

QUESTIONS

1. Which of the following is NOT a category into which rocks can be grouped?
   a. sedimentary
   b. rudimentary
   c. metamorphic
   d. igneous

2. Which of the following is a type of igneous rock?
   a. granite
   b. limestone
   c. slate
   d. marble

3. How are igneous rocks formed?
   a. They are formed when sediment is moved from one place to another.
   b. They are formed when pieces of sediment settle in layers.
   c. They are formed when magma cools.
   d. They are formed when metamorphic rock is changed by great pressure.

4. Which two of the following are metamorphic rocks?
   a. slate and granite
   b. marble and basalt
   c. marble and gneiss
   d. limestone and shale

5. What material can make up sediment?
   a. shell
   b. sand
   c. mud
   d. all of the above

6. Which is a type of sedimentary rock?
   a. gneiss
   b. shale
   c. slate
   d. all of the above

7. What is magma?
   a. sediment
   b. minerals
   c. melted rock
   d. marble

8. Rocks are classified by composition and
   a. height.
   b. weight.
   c. texture.
   d. width.

Chimpanzees

Chimpanzees are our closest relatives in the animal kingdom. Chimpanzees are considered apes, like gorillas, orangutans, and gibbons. They are not classified as monkeys. One difference between monkeys and apes is that apes have no tails. Chimpanzees have no tails. They are extremely intelligent and resourceful, and they are social creatures.

Chimpanzees are found in West Africa. They live in the forests and the mountains, where there are very leafy trees and brush. Chimps walk on the ground and climb in the trees. They do not walk upright like humans, though. They "knuckle-walk," which from far away may be mistaken as walking on their hands and feet, but if you look closely you can see they are actually walking on the first knuckle joint of their fingers.

Chimpanzees are diurnal, which means they are awake during the day and they sleep at night. They are *omnivores*. They eat about 200 kinds of leaves and fruit, as well as honey, birds' eggs, birds, fish, and roots. They also like to eat insects, including beetles, termites, and ants.

Being social creatures, chimpanzees live in groups. These groups can number up to 50 chimps. They consist of male and female chimps, plus their offspring. The male chimp is dominant in these groups (meaning he is the one in charge). A grown male chimp can weigh between 135 and 150 pounds, and can be about four to five feet tall. A grown female is slightly smaller. A chimp's life expectancy is about 50 years. A female chimp will give birth to one baby at a time, and the baby chimp is totally dependent on the mother up until the age of about five. Chimps also groom each other; this is a social activity as well as to keep themselves clean. Chimps will pick fleas, ticks, and other parasites off each other, then as a bonus they will eat the bugs they find.

Chimpanzees are very smart. They even use tools. One thing they do is go "fishing" for termites, and they do this in old rotted tree trunks, not in the water. First they grab a long, thin stick with no leaves on it. Then they put the stick in a hole of a tree trunk. They keep the stick in there for a few seconds. When they pull the stick out, they can lick the termites off. To a chimp this is a tasty treat. Chimps also use rocks and sticks to crack open nuts. And when a chimp can't reach his head in a hole to drink the water in there, he will use leaves to soak up the water. Then he squeezes the water into his mouth.

Leopards *prey upon* chimpanzees, so chimps have to watch out for these big cats, but poachers and traders are a bigger problem for chimpanzees. Chimps belong living free and in the wild, so there is a great need for *conservation*.

QUESTIONS

1. What is one way in which chimps do not use tools?
   a. They use rocks to crack open a nut.
   b. They use sticks to fish for termites.
   c. They use sticks to draw in the sand.
   d. They use leaves to soak up water like a sponge.

2. What do chimpanzees like to eat?
   a. birds
   b. fish
   c. termites
   d. all of the above

3. What does *prey upon* mean?
   a. play with
   b. hunt and eat
   c. are eaten by
   d. catch and release

4. What does *omnivore* mean?
   a. eating only animals
   b. eating only plants
   c. eating plants and animals
   d. chewing with your mouth open

5. What is a difference between monkeys and apes?
   a. Apes have no tail.
   b. Apes walk upright.
   c. Monkeys climb trees.
   d. all of the above

6. Why do chimpanzees groom each other?
   a. as a social activity to keep each other company
   b. for good hygiene to keep each other clean
   c. both **a** and **b**
   d. neither **a** nor **b**

7. Why are chimpanzees considered smart?
   a. because they eat leaves
   b. because they use tools
   c. because they knuckle-walk
   d. all of the above

8. Based on the passage, what do you think *conservation* means?
   a. preserving land and animals so the animals can live in the wild
   b. poaching and trading animals
   c. getting rid of all the leopards
   d. doing nothing about the animals

Passage Six

The Fox and the Crow

Once upon a time there was a black crow who lived in the forest. One bright and sunny day he was flying around searching for food. He usually ate very uninteresting things—worms, bugs, maybe a grasshopper or some corn. Well on this day he *spied* some picnickers under a nearby tree. He sat on a branch and looked at all the good food that they had.

He noticed that the people were starting to pack up their food. A nice, big, fat piece of yellow cheese had fallen off the picnic blanket and the crow eyed it hungrily. The people left the forest, leaving behind the cheese. The crow swooped down out of the tree and grabbed the big piece of cheese in his beak. He held the cheese tightly in his beak. It was too big to eat in one gulp. He would have to put it down and peck at it.

But first, he was so happy that he swooped in circles in the air, yelling "My cheese! My cheese! I got the cheese!" Some other animals in the forest heard him. His voice was a bit muffled from having the cheese in his beak, but the animals still understood him. They watched as he landed lightly on a tree branch.

The bunny hopped under the tree, looked up at the crow and said "Please Mr. Crow, won't you share that fine looking piece of cheese?"

"No," answered the crow in his muffled voice. "It's all mine. I found it and I get to eat it." So the bunny hopped away. A young fawn came up under the tree and asked politely if the crow wouldn't mind sharing with her.

"I'm ever so hungry," she said. But the crow just mumbled out "No!"

The fawn hung her head down and walked away *dejectedly*. After the fawn had left, a *sly* fox snuck up to the tree.

"Mr. Crow!" said the fox gaily. "I'm so happy to see you!" The crow was surprised to hear him say that.

"Why?" mumbled the crow, barely coherent with the cheese still in his beak.

"Why, because I heard, that of all the birds of the forest, you have the most beautiful singing voice. I would love to hear you sing!"

"Really?" asked the crow. He had thought the fox was after his cheese, but obviously this fox was too smart and had very good taste. This crow was very vain, and believed that the fox truly thought that he had the most beautiful singing voice.

"Oh yes," said the fox. "I was hoping you would sing me a song. Nice and loud and clear! It would make my day!"

The crow was so conceited that he immediately opened his mouth to sing a loud song, forgetting momentarily about the cheese, and the cheese fell out of his mouth. The second it hit the ground, the fox gobbled it up and ran away laughing.

"Oh, thank you, Mr. Crow!" he shouted as ran. "Good-bye!" And the crow sat alone on his branch, with no cheese for his lunch.

QUESTIONS

1. In the context of the story, what does the word *spied* mean?
   a. scared
   b. noticed
   c. heard
   d. surprised

2. How does the fox get the cheese at the end of the story?
   a. He chases the crow.
   b. He captures the crow.
   c. He tricks the crow.
   d. He sings for the crow.

3. Who was the first animal to ask for some cheese?
   a. the crow
   b. the fawn
   c. the bunny
   d. the fox

4. After reading the story, what do you think the word *dejectedly* means?
   a. happily
   b. gaily
   c. angrily
   d. miserably

5. How did the crow's voice sound with the cheese in it?
   a. muffled
   b. clear
   c. distinct
   d. hilarious

6. What does *sly* mean?
   a. funny
   b. tricky
   c. kind
   d. happy

7. Why was the fox really happy to see the crow?
   a. He really loved the crow's voice.
   b. He was happy at the idea of stealing the cheese.
   c. He wanted to hang out with the crow.
   d. The crow owed him money.

8. What food didn't the crow usually eat?
   a. worms
   b. bugs
   c. corn
   d. fish

Passage Seven

SINCE THIS PARAGRAPH includes some elevated vocabulary for a fourth grader, a list is provided for you before the passage.

Vocabulary:
1. *Antiseptics*—germ killers
2. *Dilute*—to add water and make weaker

Alexander Fleming

Alexander Fleming was born in Scotland on August 6, 1881. He was a farmer's son. When he was 13 he moved to England. He worked as a shipping clerk for four years. Then he went to medical school. In 1906, he started studying vaccines with another doctor.

Alexander was a captain in World War I. He was in the Medical Corps. He took care of soldiers with infected wounds. He used *antiseptics* to kill all the germs. The antiseptics killed the germs, but they also hurt the white blood cells of the soldier. White blood cells help your body fight off sickness. Alexander became very interested in the study of blood and antiseptics. He wanted to find a substance that would kill germs but not hurt the body.

After the war he worked in a lab growing deadly bacteria and for many years tested substance after substance against these bacteria. Then in 1928 he noticed one of his bacteria cultures had gotten mold on it. He was about to throw it out when he noticed all the bacteria, in a ring around the mold, had disappeared. There was an entire bacteria-free circle around the mold. He did more experiments and found that the mold still killed the bacteria even when it was *diluted* 800 times.

This mold was a bacteria killer, or *antibiotic*. Alexander named it penicillin. It even killed the bacteria that caused pneumonia without hurting white blood cells. In 1939, two British doctors made pure penicillin. By 1943 American and English factories were making a lot of penicillin. Alexander won many awards for his good work. In 1945 he won the Nobel Prize for medicine. Since his discovery, millions and millions of lives have been saved, thanks to penicillin. Alexander Fleming died on March 11, 1955.

1. What did Alexander do for four years before going to medical school?
    a. He was a farmer.
    b. He was a shipping clerk.
    c. He was a biologist.
    d. He was in the army.

2. During the war, how did Alexander take care of the soldiers' wounds?
    a. with antibiotics
    b. with white blood cells
    c. with antiseptics
    d. with penicillin

3. What helps your body fight off sickness?
    a. white blood cells
    b. red blood cells
    c. bacteria
    d. mold

4. What does *antibiotic* mean?
    a. bacteria
    b. bacteria killer
    c. substance
    d. antiseptic

5. In 1939, who made pure penicillin?
    a. Dr. Fleming
    b. two British doctors
    c. the American factories
    d. none of the above

6. In what year did Alexander Fleming win the Nobel Prize?
    a. 1939
    b. 1943
    c. 1945
    d. 1955

7. What was Alexander in the war?
    a. Private
    b. Lieutenant
    c. Major
    d. Captain

8. How did Alexander know that the mold killed the bacteria?
   a. All the bacteria, in a ring around the mold, had disappeared.
   b. All the mold had disappeared.
   c. The bacteria and the mold turned all different colors.
   d. He took a guess.

Passage Eight

The Magic Show

"**There's nothing to** do," sighed Elena. She and her grandmother had just finished lunch. Grandmother was putting the mayonnaise, mustard, and dill pickles back into the refrigerator.

"What do you mean, 'there's nothing to do'?" Grandmother chided gently. She noticed that Elena looked a little sad.

"Well, I finished reading my book, and now I don't have anything to do." Elena didn't look like herself; her normally cheerful face looked *gloomy*. "Hmmm," pondered Grandmother. "What kind of book was it? It must have been a good one. You read it very quickly."

"It was really interesting. Here, look," said Elena as she handed Grandmother the book. The book was titled *Home Brewed Magic*. It was a collection of magic tricks written by Harriet Houdini. Ms. Houdini was Elena's favorite author. Elena had every book Ms. Houdini had ever written. She had even met her at one of the library's "Author Talks" last year. Elena warned Grandmother, "You can look at the cover, but don't peek inside. I may want to stump you with one of the tricks someday!"

Grandmother studied the book. The front cover featured a dark room with a table in its center. On the table was a single, lit candle. The flame from the candle filled the room with an eerie glow. The back cover listed things people said about the book, such as, "Ms. Houdini weaves her spell once again!" and "Another magical masterpiece by Ms. Houdini."

Grandmother's mouth curved into a slow, thoughtful smile. "I have an idea," she said, still holding the book. "Why don't you put on a magic show? You can use some of the tricks in this book."

Elena liked Grandmother's idea. But one thing troubled her. "I can't do a whole magic show just for one person," she said. "That wouldn't be much fun."

To this, Grandmother waved her hand and shook her head. "Don't worry," she reassured Elena. "I've got at least a dozen friends who would love to see your magic show." Grandmother began to count them off, "There's Madge and Cornelia—Arnold, Dekum, and Floyd—"

"Okay, okay," giggled Elena. The names of Grandmother's friends made her chuckle. "I'll get started, then." Reaching for the book, Elena turned to the index to look for the section called "Magic-Trick Necessities."

"Put together a list of what you'll need," Grandmother said. "Then we can make a trip to the store. In the meantime, I've got some phone calls to make."

QUESTIONS

1. In this story, Elena feels gloomy. *Gloomy* means
   a. puzzled.
   b. hopeful.
   c. excited.
   d. unhappy.

2. Where does this story take place?
   a. a kitchen
   b. a bedroom
   c. a library
   d. a dark room

3. Which of these is a FACT in this story?
   a. Elena lives with Grandmother.
   b. Elena met Harriet Houdini.
   c. Elena is skilled at magic tricks.
   d. Elena ate dill pickles for lunch.

4. Which of these is the best summary for the story?
   a. Elena and Grandmother enjoyed lunch together.
   b. Elena learns how to do magic tricks by herself.
   c. Grandmother invites her friends to a magic show.
   d. Grandmother helps Elena find something to do.

5. When Ms. Houdini writes another book, Elena will probably
   a. write her a fan letter.
   b. give it to Grandmother.
   c. read it as soon as she can.
   d. get a copy at the library.

6. What is *Home Brewed Magic* mainly about?
   a. the history of magic tricks
   b. magic around the world
   c. how to do magic tricks
   d. making magic with candles

7. Which of these is an OPINION in this story?
   a. *Home Brewed Magic* is an interesting book.
   b. *Home Brewed Magic* is written by Ms. Houdini.
   c. Elena has copies of all of Ms. Houdini's books.
   d. The magic show was Grandmother's idea.

8. In this story, the reader can tell that Grandmother is
   a. proud.
   b. healthy.
   c. shy.
   d. kind.

Passage Nine

The Hair Cut

When I was a kid, my dad was my barber. Since he didn't like to waste time, he would usually warm up the electric clippers while my brothers and I waited in line for our haircuts. When the clippers were ready to go, *buzz!* Those clippers could have trimmed hedges; they cut through our hair like a hot knife going through butter.

Before I go on with this story, I should also tell you that I practically worshipped my brother Kris. Kris was so cool. After all, he was a *teenager*, and anything he did, I wanted to do. If Kris was riding his bike, *I* wanted to ride my bike. If Kris was jumping off a bridge, *I* wanted to jump off a bridge. If Kris was going to breathe oxygen in and carbon dioxide out, *I* wanted to . . . Well, you get the picture.

One summer day, Dad told Kris, my two younger brothers, and me that it was once again time for our haircuts. I was the first. *Buzz*—One minute I had hair; the next minute I had none. I didn't worry about it because I knew that my hair would eventually grow back. So there I was, a mere nine years old and completely bald.

Kris was next. *Buzz*—Dad shaved one side of his head. *Buzz*—Dad shaved the other side of his head.

"Hold on a minute, Dad," Kris said. "Let me look in the mirror."

At this point, Kris had one big ridge of hair sticking straight up on the center of his head. The dark brown ridge stretched from his forehead all the way to the back of his neck. Kris rubbed one hand through his narrow ridge of hair.

"Cool! Can I leave it like this, Dad?" Kris asked.

"It's *your* head," Dad chuckled.

"All right!" Kris exclaimed. "It's the new fashion!"

That's how cool Kris was; he could invent a new fashion, just like that.

My two younger brothers got haircuts just like Kris's, and then all three of them started running around like wild animals—whooping and hollering.

They had cool haircuts; they were "in." But I was left out. All of my hair had been cut off—I couldn't just grow it back and get another haircut . . . or could I?

Later that day, if you walked past our house, you would have seen four boys with strange haircuts running around and having fun.

How is that possible, you ask? A closer look at one of the boys would reveal something unusual about his hair. In fact, you would see that it was not hair at all, but a raccoon tail taped to the top of the boy's head!

You might ask the boy, "Why is there a raccoon tail taped to your head?"

And the boy would reply, "It's the newest fashion!"

QUESTIONS

1. Who cuts the brothers' hair?
   a. the town barber
   b. the older brother
   c. the new neighbor
   d. the boys' father

2. Why does the boy telling the story think Kris is so cool?
   a. Kris enjoys acting foolish.
   b. Kris jumps off bridges.
   c. Kris has brothers.
   d. Kris is a teenager.

3. The second paragraph is mostly about how the boy
   a. wanted to go to the barber.
   b. felt about his older brother.
   c. spent his summer vacation.
   d. worried about being left out.

4. Why did Kris ask to leave his hair the way it was?
    a. He thought it looked good.
    b. He wanted his hair long.
    c. He disliked his dad's haircuts.
    d. He hoped to scare people.

5. Which of the following is a FACT from the story?
    a. He had four brothers.
    b. He was nine years old.
    c. He wore a raccoon hat.
    d. He got his haircut last.

6. At the end of the story, the boy feels
    a. embarrassed to be watched.
    b. hurt to be left out and ignored.
    c. happy to be part of the group.
    d. tired from all of the excitement.

7. What was Kris's new fashion?
    a. a shaved head
    b. a bright T-shirt
    c. a ridge of hair
    d. a raccoon's tail

Passage Ten

Mountain Biking

Bicycles have always been popular forms of transportation. They are used for work and play. They are found on city streets, small towns, and even in the mountains. The first mountain bikes were built in 1975. They were made to ride over rocky *terrain*. In order to handle the rocks and bumps on these trails, bicycles were built with heavy, balloon-like tires. They only had one speed, and they had coaster brakes.

As this new sport grew, bicycle makers came up with ways to make mountain bikes lighter, safer, and easier to ride. They made the wheels smaller and the tires knobbier so they had a better grip. They made the frames stronger and added a system that allowed the rider to change gears.

Many modern mountain bikes have *suspension systems* that take out a lot of the bumps and jolts. This gives the rider a much smoother ride. The brakes have also been improved so that riders can slow down and stop more safely. All in all, these changes make mountain bikes much easier to ride.

Today, more mountain bikes are sold than any other type of bicycle. There are mountain bike races and clubs. If you ride a mountain bike or if you are thinking of becoming a mountain bike rider, here are some suggestions to make your biking safer and more enjoyable:

1. Always wear a helmet. Helmets can prevent head injuries.
2. Bicycle gloves and sunglasses make riding more comfortable.
3. Be alert. Always know the ground you are covering.
4. Carry tools, a bicycle pump, and a spare tube so you can fix a flat tire.
5. If you're not sure that a trail is safe, get off your bike and walk.
6. Bring along a map if you're not familiar with the area where you are riding.
7. Always ride with another person.

There are many ways to get even more information about mountain biking. There are books and magazines about mountain biking. You can contact a bicycle club such as the *International Mountain Bike Association*. Your local bike shop owner may even be able to help you. You will find that mountain biking helps improve your health, lets you enjoy the beauty of nature, and is just plain fun!

QUESTIONS

1. Mountain bikes were invented
   a. to deliver mail to people.
   b. to ride on busy city streets.
   c. to ride over bumpy roads and trails.
   d. to use as transportation to work.

2. Mountain bikes have a better grip on the road because they have knobby tires and
   a. smaller frames.
   b. smaller wheels.
   c. larger seats.
   d. larger frames.

3. Riding a mountain bike on bumpy roads is made smoother because they have a
   a. good braking system.
   b. suspension system.
   c. curved handlebar.
   d. safety record.

4. Which of the following is NOT a statement about the benefits of mountain biking?
   a. You will enjoy improved health.
   b. Mountain biking is lots of fun.
   c. You get to see the beauty of nature while riding.
   d. You will get wet when it rains.

5. In this passage, the words *suspension systems* means the same as
   a. springs that let the wheels move up and down over bumps.
   b. brakes that allow a bike rider to stop more safely.
   c. hooks for hanging your mountain bike on the wall.
   d. balloon-like tires that grip the road.

6. In this passage, the word *terrain* means the same as
   a. trail maps that guide riders through the woods.
   b. hills, rocks, ditches, and other natural features.
   c. a mountain bike club for groups of riders.
   d. a helmet worn by a mountain bike rider.

7. According to the passage, it is always a good idea to
   a. set out early in the morning.
   b. carry a first aid kit.
   c. ride with a partner.
   d. drink lots of water.

8. Which of the following is the best summary of the passage?
   a. Safety is the most important part of mountain biking; sunglasses and gloves make biking more comfortable; new suspension systems help when riding on bumpy mountain roads; first aid kits are important to carry on trips.
   b. Mountain bike clubs are good for groups of riders; bicycle pumps and spare tubes are important safety features; trail maps are good for beginners.
   c. Mountain bikes were invented in 1975; mountain bikes are good ways to ride to work or play; mountain bikes have coaster brakes; mountain bikes are safer than regular bicycles; there are many safety features to remember.
   d. Mountain bikes were invented in 1975 and then the sport started to grow; there were many new features added that made mountain biking safe and fun; safety is always a good idea; there are many ways to get good information about mountain biking.

Passage Eleven

THIS FABLE FROM old Mexico is about a dog and his wild-dog brother, the coyote.

The Dog and the Coyote

Long ago in the Mexican desert, there lived a dog and a chicken farmer. One day, the farmer heard the chickens clucking and squawking and making a terrible *racket*. The farmer went to the chicken coop to see what was happening. Outside the coop, a wolf was pacing. It looked hungrily at the farmer's fat chickens. Nearby, the dog, which was supposed to be protecting the chickens, was sound asleep. In a rage, the farmer chased away the wolf and then shouted at the dog. "What a useless dog you are!"

The dog crept into the desert, ashamed of himself. For hours he wandered around the desert, occasionally stopping to rest beside a cactus or yucca plant. He was looking for something to eat when he heard Coyote's howl. Following the sound, the dog found Coyote. He was preparing to *hurdle* a tall cactus plant.

"Are you crazy?" the dog said to Coyote. "You cannot jump over a cactus!"

The Coyote replied, "Just watch me."

With that, Coyote leaped up and landed right on top of the cactus. Covered in thorns and howling loudly, he fell to the ground.

The dog took pity on Coyote, for he was in great pain. For the next couple of hours, the dog carefully pulled each thorn out of Coyote. When the dog was finished, Coyote was indeed thankful.

"What a fine dog you are!" Coyote said to the dog. "And what kindness you have shown me! I must return your kindness," said Coyote.

"I am neither fine nor deserving of your thanks," said the dog to Coyote, "for I am a useless watchdog."

The dog proceeded to tell Coyote what had happened at the farm that morning. More than anything, the dog wanted to make things right with the farmer again. "I have a plan," said Coyote, "and I believe it will help you."

Back at the farm that night, Coyote slipped into the chicken coop. The chickens cackled and squawked and disturbed the farmer. He put down his book, grabbed an old lantern, and went down to the chicken coop. The chickens were making a terrible fuss. The farmer threw open the coop gate just in time to see the dog chase Coyote from the pen.

"What a fine dog you are!" said the farmer this time.

Coyote ran to a bluff overlooking the farm and laughed and howled at the moon.

QUESTIONS

1. How did the dog feel at the end of the story?
   a. surprised
   b. nervous
   c. excited
   d. pleased

2. How did Coyote feel at the end of the story?
   a. proud
   b. curious
   c. amused
   d. calm

3. Information in the story suggests that the dog wanted
   a. the chickens to squawk quietly.
   b. the farmer to be proud of him.
   c. the coyote to leave him alone.
   d. the desert to be his new home.

4. In the future, the dog and the coyote will probably
   a. live and work on the farm.
   b. eat the farmer's chickens.
   c. continue to help each other.
   d. make friends with the wolf.

5. What was the last thing the farmer did before he praised the dog?
   a. He went down to the coop.
   b. He opened the coop's gate.
   c. He saw Coyote being chased.
   d. He grabbed an old lantern.

6. In this story, to make a *racket* is to make a
   a. bad choice.
   b. good deal.
   c. sharp tool.
   d. loud noise.

7. Which of these is a FACT in the story?
   a. The coyote was a clever animal.
   b. The dog had grown up on the farm.
   c. The farmer was a chicken farmer.
   d. The chickens were much too noisy.

8. In this story, the word *hurdle* means
   a. throw.
   b. push.
   c. leap.
   d. shout.

9. Which of these is the best summary of this story?
   a. A dog who was scolded for being useless goes into the desert and makes a friend who helps him solve his problem.
   b. A farmer gets angry with his dog, sends the dog into the desert, and tells him to never come back to the farm.
   c. A coyote with a funny sense of humor plays tricks on a farmer and tries to scare his chickens out of their coop.
   d. A coop of chickens is always being frightened by wild animals until their watchdog learns how to do his job better.

Passage Twelve

What Will Lucy Choose?

Lucy hummed cheerfully to herself as she walked to the bookstore. Her birthday was only a week away. She was humming—happy birthday to me, happy birthday to me.

Every year, Grandpa and Grandma Chavez gave Lucy a gift. They let her pick out any magazine she wanted. Lucy liked choosing a new magazine each year. Lucy had chosen science, puzzle, and pet magazines in the past. This year, she wanted something new. She was curious about nature and the outdoors. "Maybe a camping magazine would be fun," Lucy thought. She looked through the bookstore's magazines.

"Ah-ha! This one looks good," Lucy said aloud. She grabbed the June copy of *Trail Mix* and turned to the *Table* of Contents.

Trail Mix—The Magazine for Young Campers
June 2000 Vol. 33 No. 4
Table of Contents

Articles

Departments

Fiction

Comics

Readers' Voices

Coming Next Month

Exciting Night Hikes

Dangerous Critters

Award-Winning Campfires

On the Front Cover

Mount Shasta at sunrise, photography by Mary E. Groh.

Visit our website at www.trailmix.com/kids.

Join Young Campers of America. Get a free subscription to *Trail Mix*, a membership card, and a *Trail Mix* T-shirt. To become a member, call 800-555-3891, Monday–Friday, 8 A.M.–7 P.M. Eastern Standard Time.

Trail Mix is published monthly by O.O.A., the Organization for Outdoor Activity, Washington, DC 20036.

1. In this passage, the word *table* means
   a. book.
   b. photo.
   c. list.
   d. cover.

2. In this passage, the first thing Lucy did was
   a. grab a copy of *Trail Mix*.
   b. look at magazines.
   c. walk to a bookstore.
   d. go camping and hiking.

3. Which part of the magazine would contain letters from campers?
   a. Comics
   b. Readers' Voices
   c. Coming Next Month
   d. Departments

4. "Arrow Mountain," "Secrets in the Sand," and "The Hidden Cave" are listed together because they are all
   a. photos.
   b. articles.
   c. trails.
   d. stories.

5. Next year, Lucy will probably
   a. move to the mountains.
   b. choose a new magazine.
   c. cancel the subscription.
   d. send a letter to *Trail Mix*.

6. This passage is mostly about
   a. where the magazine is made.
   b. who reads the magazine.
   c. what is in the magazine.
   d. why the magazine is costly.

7. You might be able to find information about camping clothes on page
   a. 3.
   b. 9.
   c. 12.
   d. 18.

8. Which part of the magazine contains something to help you learn about maps?
   a. Coming Next Month
   b. Readers' Voices
   c. Departments
   d. Articles

Passage Thirteen

Dee Dee Jonrowe

Dee Dee Jonrowe is a sled dog racer. She has been mushing since she was seventeen. At her home in Willow, Alaska, she trains her own race dogs. In fact, she trains forty Alaskan huskies at once. The dogs begin their race training when they are just puppies. Sled dogs need about two years of training. Then they are finally ready for a race.

Sled dog races are popular in Alaska, where snow covers the ground for much of the year. Some of these races have unusual names. One race is called "Beargrease." Another is called "Nenana Comeback." And then there's the "Iditarod." The Iditarod is Alaska's most famous sled-dog race, and it has an interesting history.

The story of the Iditarod dates back to 1925 in the town of Nome, Alaska. Some very sick people in town needed medicine. People tried and tried to get medicine into town, but the weather was terrible. There was a blizzard. No one was able to come or go safely. Finally, a team of sled dogs saved the day. The dogs were the only ones able to carry the medicine into town. The Iditarod celebrates this event. The race is over 1,500 miles long. It goes all the way from Anchorage to Nome. For most contestants, it takes ten days to finish.

Dee Dee Jonrowe has raced in eighteen Iditarods. She is very proud of her dogsled team and the fact that together they have won second place twice. In 1996, Jonrowe was injured in a car accident. She worried she might never be able to race again, but she refused to give up. Only four months after the accident, Jonrowe and some of her "best friends" finished yet another Iditarod.

1. Read this sentence from the first paragraph of the article.
    She has been mushing since she was seventeen.

    Based on the article, what does *mushing* mean?
    a. sled dog racing
    b. a dog's way of speaking
    c. a type of dog food
    d. a type of snow hiking

2. Why did the author probably write this article?
    a. to tell the reader about the town of Nome, Alaska
    b. to introduce a sled dog racer and a race to the reader
    c. to teach the reader about the lives of Alaskan huskies
    d. to explain to the reader how difficult a sled dog race is

3. Think about the story of the first Iditarod race. Arrange these events in the order in which they took place in the story.
    1. The Iditarod Race was celebrated.
    2. Medicine was needed in Nome.
    3. A team of sled dogs saved the day.
    4. People tried to bring medicine into Nome.

    a. 3, 1, 2, 4
    b. 1, 2, 4, 3
    c. 2, 1, 4, 3
    d. 2, 4, 3, 1

4. Based on the article, which of the following statements is NOT true?
    a. Jonrowe began sled-dog racing as a teenager.
    b. Jonrowe has been in over a dozen Iditarods.
    c. Jonrowe enjoys training more than racing.
    d. Jonrowe has won second place at the Iditarod.

5. Based on the article, why did Jonrowe worry that she might never race again?
    a. She became terribly ill in 1996.
    b. She was hurt in a car accident.
    c. She could not improve her racing time.
    d. She had lost some of her "best friends."

6. Which set of words gives the best description of Jonrowe?
    a. quiet and intelligent
    b. adventurous and funny
    c. worried and brave
    d. proud and determined

7. Based on the article, who are Jonrowe's best friends?
   a. the people of Nome, Alaska
   b. contestants
   c. other sled dog racers
   d. sled dogs

Passage Fourteen

Mask Traditions

You will need to know the following words as you read the story:

> *traditions:* handed-down beliefs
> *Hopi:* a North American Indian people of Arizona
> *Kwakiutl:* a North American Indian people of western Canada
> *framework:* stiff part that gives something its shape
> *plywood:* thin layers of wood pressed together

Masks play an important part in traditions around the world. For some people, masks are a part of their beliefs and customs. Masks might be worn to mark an important event or to celebrate a rich harvest. Masks might also be worn to call for a change in weather or to celebrate a child's passing into adulthood. No matter what the reason, masks have been used for thousands of years. They reflect the traditions, arts, and natural materials of an area.

In North America, the most familiar masks are probably Halloween masks. Children "trick or treat" from house to house, wearing masks to disguise themselves. They pretend to be ghosts and monsters. They collect candy from neighbors in exchange for not playing tricks.

Long ago in North America, Native Americans also wore masks. They had their own special mask traditions. Although some of these traditions have not survived, the Kwakiutl Indians and the Hopi Indians are working to keep their mask traditions alive.

Kwakiutl artists carve their masks from red cedar wood and decorate them with bark or animal hide. Many Kwakiutl masks have moving parts. One such mask, the thunderbird, represents a frightening forest spirit. The mask is quite large—up to eight feet long. It has a huge beak that snaps open and shut. The dancer who wears it operates the beak by pulling cords.

The Hopi make their masks out of leather. A framework of plywood is added so that ears, noses, snouts, horns, and other decorations can be attached. Because the Hopi were great farmers, some of their masks, called *kachina* masks, relate to the seasons and the harvest. Symbols of corn, clouds, or rainbows often decorate the *kachina* masks. These symbols represent spirits that call for rain or sun.

When traditions such as the Kwakiutl and Hopi masks are kept alive, it is a great benefit for all people. These traditions teach us a lot about history, values, customs, and beliefs.

QUESTIONS

1. Read this sentence from the article.
    Masks might be worn to mark an important event or to celebrate a rich harvest.

    In this sentence, what does the word *rich* mean?
    a. expensive
    b. joyful
    c. plentiful
    d. pleasant

2. Why did the author probably write this article?
    a. to help people to enjoy traditions like Halloween
    b. to show people how to wear masks
    c. to tell people about some ways masks are used
    d. to encourage people to wear scary masks

3. How are Kwakiutl masks made?
    a. They are carved from cedar wood.
    b. They are carved from plywood.
    c. They are made from leather.
    d. They are made from pieces of bark glued together.

4. Why do symbols of the harvest decorate *kachina* masks?
    a. Harvest symbols are easy to understand.
    b. The Hopi Indians once lived in the forest.
    c. The Kwakiutl Indians were farmers.
    d. The Hopi Indians were farmers.

5. What happens to a *kachina* mask BEFORE its decorations can be attached?
   a. A plywood framework is added.
   b. A spirit must call for rain or sun.
   c. The bark is thoroughly dried.
   d. The dancer makes sure that the mask fits.

6. Read this sentence from the article.
   It has a huge beak that snaps open and shut. The dancer operates the beak with cords.

   What does the word *operates* mean?
   a. attaches
   b. moves
   c. covers
   d. studies

7. Why does the author think it is important to keep traditions alive?
   a. They make our holidays interesting.
   b. They show the history of disguises.
   c. They help us learn about beliefs and customs.
   d. They provide valuable entertainment.

Passage Fifteen

A Taste of Chocolate

Chocolate is a favorite treat for young and old. People worldwide enjoy the taste of chocolate in candies, cakes, cookies, or drinks. Nothing beats a cup of hot cocoa on a cold winter day.

Chocolate comes from the seeds, or beans, of the cacao tree. Strangely, we call these beans cocoa beans, not cacao beans. This was probably a spelling mistake made long ago. No matter how you spell it, life before chocolate is hard to imagine.

Where Have You Bean All My Life?

The Aztecs of Mexico grew cocoa beans at least six hundred years ago. The bean was an important part of their culture. They believed the beans gave them wisdom and they made a rich drink from them. They also used the beans to buy other things.

In 1528, cocoa beans made their way from Mexico to Spain. Over the next several hundred years, the beans grew very popular. They spread to

Italy, Austria, France, and England. Today, the people of Europe and the United States eat most of the world's chocolate.

From the Tropics

The cacao tree grows best in a warm climate. Most cocoa beans come from the west coast of Africa. Workers cut melon-sized pods from the cacao trees and scoop out the cocoa beans. They pile the beans under banana leaves and let them sit for about a week. Then the beans are dried in the sun. Finally, workers bag the dried beans for shipment.

To the Factory

The cocoa beans arrive at the factory where workers clean and roast them. Then they hull the beans, removing their shells. What is left is called a nib. Machines grind the nibs into a dark brown liquid. All chocolate comes from this liquid.

More than Just Chips

There are several kinds of chocolate. How many do you know?

Unsweetened chocolate, or baking chocolate, is not sweet at all. It is very bitter. It must be mixed with sugar and other ingredients to make treats like brownies, cakes, frostings, and sauces.

Bittersweet chocolate is both bitter and sweet. It has some sugar and cocoa butter in it. We often use it to make candy, cookies, and cakes. It is Europe's favorite chocolate.

Semisweet chocolate is sweeter still. It contains sugar, cocoa butter, and vanilla. It is usually sold as chips or morsels that are used in candy, fudge, and cookies.

Milk chocolate is the sweetest of all. It contains sugar, extra cocoa butter, and milk. Most candy bars use milk chocolate. This is the United States's favorite chocolate.

Cocoa is a reddish-brown powder made from a hard block of cocoa butter. Hot chocolate, cakes, ice cream, and many other food products contain cocoa.

1. Under which heading can you find the history of the cocoa bean?
   a. "Where Have You Bean All My Life?"
   b. "From the Tropics"
   c. "To the Factory"
   d. "More than Just Chips"

2. Based on the article, what is one way the Aztecs used the cocoa bean?
   a. They used it as medicine.
   b. They used it as money.
   c. They used it to make cookies.
   d. They used it like sugar.

3. Why did the author write the article "A Taste of Chocolate?"
   a. to tell readers some facts about chocolate
   b. to show how delicious chocolate is
   c. to prove that chocolate is healthful
   d. to explain why chocolate is popular

4. Read the paragraph under the heading, "From the Tropics." Based on the paragraph, which sentence is true?
   a. Cacao trees do not need water to grow.
   b. The pods are smaller than the beans.
   c. Bananas and cocoa come from the same tree.
   d. The beans grow inside the pods.

5. Which part of the bean is ground to make a chocolate liquid?
   a. chips
   b. shells
   c. pods
   d. nibs

6. Which of these is done LAST to the cocoa beans?
   a. The beans are dried in the sun.
   b. The beans are piled under banana leaves.
   c. The beans' shells are removed.
   d. The beans sit for about a week.

7. According to this article, what is Europe's favorite chocolate?
   a. baking chocolate
   b. bittersweet chocolate
   c. semisweet chocolate
   d. milk chocolate

Answers

1. **a.** He was born in Italy. You can find this answer in the first sentence.
2. **c.** He dreamed of being a sailor.
3. **c.** They would usually have to sail east, around Africa, to get to the Indies.
4. **d.** The Indies were India, China, and Japan.
5. **d.** "People purchased valuable jewels, cloth, clothes, animals, spices, and other exotic things over there."
6. **b.** He made his first voyage in 1492. Christopher Columbus was born in Genoa, Italy in 1451. In 1493 Columbus went back to Spain. He died in 1506 in Spain.
7. **a.** He gave them glass bead necklaces.
8. **d.** Columbus made four voyages to America in all.

1. **c.** Abraham Lincoln was born on February 12, 1809 in a little log cabin in Kentucky.
2. **c.** He loved to read and learn.
3. **c.** While he was in New Orleans he saw a slave market for the first time.
4. **c.** He was very upset to see people being treated this way.
5. **a.** Lincoln wrote the Emancipation Proclamation. This document stated that all slaves were free.
6. **c.** Stephen Douglas ran against Lincoln in the race to become president. During the war Jefferson Davis was the leader of the South. General Ulysses S. Grant led the Northern armies and Robert E. Lee led the Southern armies.
7. **d.** His nickname was "Honest Abe."
8. **b.** He was nine.

1. **d.** Adam was trying to learn how to skateboard.
2. **a.** Billy learned that even though he couldn't ride his bike at first, he had to keep trying.
3. **b.** His horn is silver. His bike is blue. And his reflectors are red.
4. **c.** In this story, it means he couldn't hold in his excitement.
5. **d.** All of the above. His mother, father and brother all cheered him on.
6. **a.** Billy scraped some of the skin off his knee.
7. **a.** Billy needed to learn how to balance on the bike so it wouldn't fall over when he was riding.
8. **d.** Billy's father's name wasn't given in the story.

1. **b.** Rudimentary is not a category.
2. **a.** Granite is a type of igneous rock.
3. **c.** This answer can be found in the second paragraph: "Igneous rocks are formed when magma cools."
4. **c.** Marble and gneiss are metamorphic rocks. Marble is formed from limestone and gneiss is made from granite.
5. **d.** Go back to the third paragraph: "Sediment can be made up of sand, shell, mud, or organic material"
6. **b.** Shale is a type of sedimentary rock. Gneiss and slate are both types of metamorphic rock.
7. **c.** Magma is melted rock.
8. **c.** Rocks are classified by composition and texture.

1. **c.** Chimps do not use sticks to draw in the sand.
2. **d.** According to the passage, chimps like to eat leaves, fruit, honey, birds and their eggs, fish, roots, and insects, including termites.
3. **b.** When the passage says that leopards prey upon chimpanzees, it means that leopards hunt and eat them.
4. **c.** *Omnivore* means eating plants and animals. You have to use your deductive reasoning here; look at what chimps eat, and you will see that the list includes both plants and animals.
5. **a.** Apes have no tail. Apes do not walk upright, and apes climb trees as well as monkeys.
6. **c.** Again, go back to the passage. "Chimps also groom each other; this is a social activity as well as to keep themselves clean."
7. **b.** You must be very careful when answering this question, especially if you chose answer **d**. The question asks, "why are chimps *considered smart?*," not "what do chimps do?" Even though chimps do all three things listed in the answer column, they are considered smart because they use tools.
8. **a.** Conservation is preserving land and animals.

1. **b.** When it says," he *spied* some picnickers," it means he noticed them.
2. **c.** The fox tricks the crow by pretending to love the crow's voice and wanting to hear him sing. The fox knew that once the crow opened his mouth the cheese would fall out.
3. **c.** The bunny was the first one to ask for some cheese.
4. **d.** The fawn hung her head after the crow said no, so you can see that she was miserable.

5. **a.** His voice sounded muffled. It is hard for someone's voice to sound clear and distinct with something in his or her mouth, and it stated in the passage that his voice sounded a bit muffled.
6. **b.** The word *sly* is most similar to tricky.
7. **b.** The fox did not love the crow's voice. He was really happy at the prospect of being able to steal the cheese.
8. **d.** In the story it says, "He usually ate very uninteresting things—worms, bugs, maybe a grasshopper or some corn." It does not mention fish.

PASSAGE SEVEN

1. **b.** He worked as a shipping clerk for four years.
2. **c.** He used antiseptics.
3. **a.** White blood cells help the body fight off sickness.
4. **b.** *Antibiotic* means bacteria killer.
5. **c.** The last paragraph states, "In 1939, two British doctors made pure penicillin."
6. **c.** He won the Nobel Prize for medicine in 1945.
7. **d.** He was a captain.
8. **a.** All the bacteria, in a ring around the mold, had disappeared. There was an entire bacteria-free circle around the mold.

PASSAGE EIGHT

1. **d.** *Gloomy* means sad or unhappy.
2. **a.** You can figure out that they are in the kitchen when you read the sentence: "She and her grandmother had just finished lunch. Grandmother was putting the mayonnaise, mustard, and dill pickles back into the refrigerator."
3. **b.** This is a fact stated in the story: "Elena had every book Ms. Houdini had ever written. She had even met her at one of the library's "Author Talks" last year." We don't know for sure if Elena actually lives with her grandmother, is skilled at the magic tricks, or if she was the one who had dill pickles for lunch.
4. **d.** The best summary for this story is to say that Elena's grandmother helps her find something to do.
5. **c.** Since Ms. Houdini was Elena's favorite author and Elena had every book Ms. Houdini had ever written, it is safe to assume that when the next book comes out Elena would read it as soon as she could.
6. **c.** You can go right back to the story: "The book was titled *Home Brewed Magic*. It was a collection of magic tricks written by Harriet Houdini."
7. **a.** This is an opinion. All the other answer choices are facts from the story.
8. **d.** You can tell by the way Grandmother helps Elena that she is kind.

PASSAGE NINE

1. **d.** The first sentence of this passage says, "When I was a kid, my dad was the barber."
2. **d.** "Kris was so cool. After all, he was a *teenager* . . . "
3. **b.** The second paragraph is mostly about how the boy felt about his older brother.
4. **a.** Just look at his reaction to seeing his hair: "Cool! Can I leave it like this, Dad?" Kris asked.
5. **b.** He states his age in the passage: "So there I was, a mere *nine years old* and completely bald."
6. **c.** It says in the story: "Later that day, if you walked past our house, you would have seen four boys with strange haircuts running around and having fun." Based upon this statement, you can see that he is happy to be part of the group.
7. **c.** Kris left a ridge of hair down the middle of his head and called it "the new fashion."

PASSAGE TEN

1. **c.** Look in the story: "They were made to ride over rocky *terrain*. In order to handle the rocks and bumps on these trails, bicycles were built with heavy, balloon-like tires."
2. **b.** "They made the wheels smaller and the tires knobbier so they had a better grip."
3. **b.** "Many modern mountain bikes have *suspension systems* that take out a lot of the bumps and jolts. This gives the rider a much smoother ride."
4. **d.** "You will find that mountain biking helps improve your health, lets you enjoy the beauty of nature, and is just plain fun!" Most people would not consider it a benefit to get wet when it rains.
5. **a.** *Suspension systems* means the same as springs that let the wheels move up and down over bumps.
6. **b.** *Terrain* means the same as hills, rocks, ditches, and other natural features.
7. **c.** "Here are some suggestions to make your biking safer and more enjoyable . . . 7. Always ride with another person."
8. **d.** A good summary would be that mountain bikes were invented in 1975 and then the sport started to grow; there were many new features added to mountain bikes that made them safe and fun; safety is always a good idea; and there are many ways to get good information about mountain biking.

1. **d.** The farmer told the dog: "What a fine dog you are!" so the dog was pleased.
2. **c.** "Coyote ran to a bluff overlooking the farm and laughed and howled at the moon." He laughed because he was amused.
3. **b.** The dog wanted the farmer to be proud of him.
4. **c.** In the future, the dog and the coyote will probably continue to help each other.
5. **c.** Look at the passage: "The farmer threw open the coop gate just in time to see the dog chase Coyote from the pen. "What a fine dog you are!" said the farmer this time."
6. **d.** To make a racket means to make a loud noise.
7. **c.** It is a fact that the farmer was a chicken farmer. We don't know for sure if the coyote was a clever animal, if the dog grew up on the farm, or if the chickens were much too noisy.
8. **c.** In this story, the word *hurdle* means leap.
9. **a.** A dog that was scolded for being useless goes into the desert and makes a friend who helps him solve his problem is the best way to summarize this story.

1. **c.** In this passage, the word *table* means list.
2. **c.** In this passage, the first thing Lucy did was walk to a bookstore.
3. **b.** The part of the magazine that would contain letters from campers is Readers' Voices.
4. **d.** "Arrow Mountain," "Secrets in the Sand," and "The Hidden Cave" are listed together because they are all fictional stories.
5. **b.** Next year, Lucy will probably choose a new magazine. We know this because in the passage it says: "Every year, Grandpa and Grandma Chavez gave Lucy a gift. They let her pick out any magazine she wanted. Lucy liked choosing a *new* magazine each year."
6. **c.** This passage is mostly about what is in the magazine. The table of contents lists what is found in the magazine.
7. **b.** You might be able to find information about camping clothes on page 9. "Suit Yourself: What to Wear" is a title for an article that would be about clothes.
8. **d.** The part of the magazine that contains something to help you learn about maps would be "Articles." This is because one of the articles is called "Map Reading for Beginners."

1. **a.** Based on the article, *mushing* means sled dog racing.
2. **b.** The author probably wrote this article to introduce a sled dog racer and a race to the reader.
3. **d.** This is the way the story would unfold: First medicine was needed in Nome. Then people tried to bring medicine into Nome. Next a team of sled dogs saved the day. And lastly, the Iditarod Race was celebrated.
4. **c.** Based on the article, the following statement is not true: Jonrowe enjoys training more than racing. The article never says this. It did say that she began sled-dog racing at 17, raced in 18 Iditarods and won second place twice.
5. **b.** Based on the article Jonrowe worried that she might never race again because she was hurt in a car accident.
6. **d.** The set of words that gives the best description of Jonrowe are *proud* and *determined*. She is proud of her accomplishments and was determined to race again after her accident.
7. **d.** Based on the article, Jonrowe's "best friends" are the sled dogs.

1. **c.** In this sentence, the word *rich* means plentiful.
2. **c.** The author probably wrote this article to tell people about some ways masks are used.
3. **a.** Look at the story: "Kwakiutl artists carve their masks from red cedar wood and decorate them with bark or animal hide."
4. **d.** Symbols of the harvest decorate *kachina* masks because the Hopi Indians were farmers.
5. **a.** "A framework of plywood is added so that ears, noses, snouts, horns, and other decorations can be attached."
6. **b.** In the sentence, the word *operates* means "moves."
7. **c.** The author thinks it is important to keep traditions alive because they teach us a lot about history, values, customs, and beliefs.

1. **a.** You'll find the history of the cocoa bean under the heading, "Where Have You Bean All My Life?"
2. **b.** "They also used the beans to buy other things," in other words, as money.
3. **a.** The author wrote the article "A Taste of Chocolate" to tell readers some facts about chocolate.
4. **d.** It is true that the beans grow inside the pods.
5. **d.** The nib is the part of the bean that is ground to make a chocolate liquid.
6. **c.** The beans' shells are removed last.
7. **b.** According to this article, Europe's favorite chocolate is bittersweet chocolate.

CHAPTER

Short and Extended Response English/ Language Arts Questions

One of the most important goals for any student is to be a good reader, and the English/Language Arts Assessment Tests measures your child's ability to read, analyze, and evaluate what is in print. On most state assessment tests, children will be asked to answer short- and extended-response questions on fiction and nonfiction passages. As students take these tests, their ability and competency in literary response and critical analysis and evaluation will be evident to teachers. Passages on this part of the test ask students to read and listen carefully, to analyze, and to relate the stories to their own lives. Students, of course, are expected to write down their own ideas and thoughts in proper, standard English.

To help your children survive this section of the test, you can buy—or borrow from your local library—children's magazines or books and encourage them to read. A good plan is to read them in tandem and then compare notes. Then, you can ask your child about the content and engage in a literary conversation. Ask factual questions or just ask for an opinion on certain ideas presented in the articles. This is good practice to get the "wheels turning." (This interpretive and evaluative skill is one your child can develop and will carry into adulthood.) Try to make these literary conversations and questions light, fun, and inviting. If you think your child has given you an incorrect answer, ask for an explanation or "literary analysis." Often, during this thinking out loud process, you and your child can discover just where and how opinions are developed.

You can also read aloud short, interesting articles you find in the paper, in magazines, or in books to your child. Your child will learn invaluable listening skills during these sessions. This will help on the test since all assessment tests have a listening section. The difference is that, on the test, your child will be encouraged to take notes from which to write a response.

Another way to help your child is to encourage him to write. Help him to write letters or thank-you notes by buying cool stationery or postcards. Or buy a fancy journal so your child can have fun recording the day's events.

If you want to help your child with vocabulary, there are many great "word of the day" books and calendars out there. Understanding vocabulary unlocks many secrets and can only help your child interpret literature or nonfiction.

Of course, the most important thing is to tell your child not to panic. A certain amount of nervousness is perfectly normal and may even help, but nothing will be gained with an all-out panic attack. Just remind your child that he has been working hard all along and has been preparing for the test, and he will do just fine.

Passage One

The Ant and the Grasshopper

Once in a meadow there lived an ant and a grasshopper. It was summer and the weather was warm and sunny. The grasshopper couldn't help but hop and play in the warm sunshine. His thoughts were only of how nice it was at that time and how he could play all day and easily get food whenever he was hungry.

On the other hand, the ant did not take time out to play. He worked very hard all day, gathering food to save for the winter. From sunrise to sunset, the ant searched the meadow far and wide for food to take back to his anthill.

"Hey ant!" said the grasshopper one day, in the beginning of the summer. "Why don't you come and play with me?"

"I can't," said the ant. "I have to gather food to save for the winter. You should be doing that as well. The days won't always be warm and sunny, and food won't always be as plentiful."

But the grasshopper paid no attention to the ant's good advice. He continued to frolic and play in the warm sunshine. One midsummer day he came across the ant again.

"Hey ant!" he said. "Won't you join me now? Take a break from your work and come play."

"I can't," replied the ant. "Summer is halfway over. I still have much food to gather. You should be doing the same thing, grasshopper."

But again the grasshopper paid no attention. He still played and jumped in the sunshine all day long.

One day, towards the end of the summer, the grasshopper noticed it was getting colder. The sun wasn't shining as much, and it was getting harder to find food. He finally realized that the ant was right. He started working day and night to collect food for the winter, but to his dismay, he found that he could barely find enough food to eat each day.

Finally, winter set in. The ant had been observing the grasshopper's actions at the end of the summer. He left his anthill and came to the spot where the grasshopper lay shivering and hungry.

"Grasshopper," said the ant, "You didn't listen to me in the beginning of the summer, nor did you listen to me in the middle of the summer. However, I have seen how hard you worked at the end, finally taking my advice. I will take you back to my anthill, and you can share my food."

"Thank you for your kindness ant," said the grasshopper. "I will try to make it up to you one day." And they went off together to the anthill.

QUESTIONS

Short Response Question 1

Why do you think the ant helped the grasshopper at the end of the story?

_____

_____

_____

Short Response Question 2

What are some ways the grasshopper could repay the ant?

_____

_____

_____

Short Response Question 3

How did the ant find food?

_____

_____

_____

Extended Response Question 1

In this passage the ant gives the grasshopper some good advice, but the grasshopper doesn't follow it until it is too late. Write an essay telling about a time someone gave you advice. Was it good advice or bad advice? Did you follow the advice or ignore it? What was the outcome?

_____

_____

_____

_____

_____

_____

_____

_____

_____

_____

Extended Response Question 2

What do you think of the behavior of the ant? Tell about how you would behave in the same situation. Next, tell about what you thought of the grasshopper's behavior. Explain how you would behave if you were the grasshopper.

_____

_____

_____

_____

_____

_____

_____

_____

Extended Response Question 3

Which one do you think is the moral of the story?
Don't put off what you should do today.
Do your work before you play.

Be sure to back up your answer.

_____

_____

_____

_____

_____

_____

_____

_____

_____

_____

Passage Two

Bats versus Birds

Although bats can fly, they are not birds. Bats are the only mammals that fly. Bats give birth to live young, and these baby bats nurse (drink milk) from their mother. Baby birds are hatched from hard-shelled eggs. The mother bird feeds the baby birds from her mouth. Sometimes she feeds them chewed-up worms. Birds hunt using their eyesight, but bats use echolocation. Echolocation is when a bat sends out a high-pitched sound, and the sound bounces back to tell the bat where things are.

Birds have feathers, but bats are covered with hair or fur. Bats have arms, hands and feet, as well as wings. Birds have wings, but no hands. Bats have teeth, but birds have beaks with no teeth. Birds have hollow bones, but bats do not. Bats are nocturnal, but most birds are awake during the day. Bats usually sleep hanging upside down.

Birds and bats are both warm-blooded vertebrates. Both birds and bats eat bugs, small animals, fruit, and nectar. Vampire bats are the only bats that drink the blood of other animals. Some birds and some bats migrate (fly to warmer climates) during the winter. Both bats and birds help in the control of insects and with seed dispersal.

QUESTIONS

Short Response Question 1

How do bats hunt?

_____

_____

_____

Short Response Question 2

What is special about the bones of birds?

_____

_____

_____

Short Response Question 3

When and how do bats sleep?

_____

_____

_____

Short Response Question 4

How do mother bats feed their babies?

_____

_____

_____

Extended Response Question 1

How do birds and bats differ?

_____

_____

_____

_____

_____

_____

_____

_____

_____

_____

Extended Response Question 2

How are birds and bats similar?

_____

_____

_____

_____

_____

_____

_____

_____

_____

Extended Response Question 3

Are you more like a bat or a bird? Explain your answer.

_____

_____

_____

_____

_____

_____

_____

_____

_____

Passage Three

Jellyfish

Jellyfish are found all over the world, from the Arctic to the tropics. But jellyfish are really not fish at all; they are invertebrates, like sea anemones and corals.

Jellyfish come in two parts, the bell and the tentacles. The bell holds the mouth and stomach, reproductive organs, and some nerves. The tentacles contain the stinging cells, which release venom. To get food, the jellyfish raises and lowers its tentacles, and when the tentacles touch something, the jellyfish stings it. The prey is then paralyzed and the jellyfish can eat it. Jellyfish have no brains, no hearing stems, and no eyes.

There are hundreds of species of jellyfish found all over the world. Most of them live in the coastal waters where there is more food.

Most jellyfish are small, with bells one to twenty inches across and short tentacles. But a few have been known to reach six feet across with tentacles that reach down over one hundred feet!

Jellyfish swim by pushing their bells in and out, but many are not strong swimmers. They are often carried by the current or the wind. Most Jellyfish are harmless and slow moving.

Jellyfish eat zooplankton (tiny sea plants and animals, like shrimp) and small fish. Some scientists thought that jellyfish just drifted until their tentacles just happened to touch something. But now they know that at least a few species of jellyfish can follow the faint chemical trails laid down by zooplankton.

Jellyfish also have creatures that eat them. They are eaten by dogfish, cod, mackerel, and ocean sunfish. They are also eaten by sea turtles. Seabirds feed on beached jellyfish and some birds, like puffins, eat them at sea.

Short Response Question 1

Are jellyfish really fish?

_____

_____

_____

Short Response Question 2

How do jellyfish move?

_____

_____

_____

Short Response Question 3

What do the tentacles of a jellyfish contain?

_____

_____

_____

Extended Response Question 1

How big are jellyfish?

_____

_____

_____

_____

_____

_____

_____

_____

Extended Response Question 2

What creatures prey upon (eat) jellyfish?

_____

_____

_____

_____

_____

_____

_____

_____

_____

Extended Response Question 3

Explain how jellyfish catch their food.

_____

_____

_____

_____

_____

_____

_____

_____

_____

Two Passages to Read and Compare

Black Bears

Black bears are large, but for the most part they are harmless. They are found across North America and live mostly in forests, but they also can be found in swamps and desert scrub. They are solitary creatures, and are very intelligent and curious.

Black bears are omnivorous. They eat plants, leaves, grasses, fruits, berries, nuts, roots, honey, carrion, insects and insect larvae, and other small mammals. They have color vision, and they can tell the difference between ripe and unripe berries just by the berries' hue (slight color differentiation). They also have a keen sense of smell.

Black bears are good at climbing trees. They are also good swimmers. They can be up to six feet long and weigh an average of 125 to 600 pounds. They have long, thick fur. Their color can range from black to light brown, silver-blue and, rarely, even white. They are flat-footed, as all bears are, and their front claws are longer than the rear claws. Black bears can run up to 35 miles per hour.

Adult black bears can go up to seven months without food during hibernation in northern ranges. A mother black bear will have two to three cubs during the winter while she is hibernating, but this will only happen every other year. The cubs will stay with the mother for about a year. The mother bear nurses her cubs. Black bears can live over 25 years in the wild.

Polar Bears

Polar bears are large, fierce predators. They live in the ice and snow around the North Pole. They are well adapted for living in their frozen, arctic environment.

Polar bears are basically carnivorous. They eat mostly seals, but occasionally they kill young walruses and beluga whales. When seals and walruses are not available, a polar bear will eat reindeer, rabbits, birds, and seaweed.

Polar bears are the largest land carnivore, and they are great hunters. They will sit patiently by a seal's breathing hole all day, and when the seal rises to take a breath the polar bear will get him in one swipe. A polar bear will also stalk seal, on the land or in the water.

Not only is a polar bear an excellent swimmer, but when stalking an animal on land, they blend in with the snow. A polar bear is even smart enough to cover its black nose with its paw.

The skin of a polar bear is black, to soak up the heat from the sun. It has white hair on its body, but also translucent guard hair to keep the water out. The fur is oily and water repellent. They have a thick layer of fat just under the skin to help keep them warm.

An adult female will hibernate in the winter and give birth to twins. The cubs nurse from their mother. The mother will build a snow den to give birth in. Adult male polar bears do not hibernate.

Polar bears can be up to ten feet long and weigh up to 1,700 pounds. A polar bear can live up to 25 years in the wild.

QUESTIONS

Extended Response Question 1

What are the similarities between black bears and polar bears?

_____

_____

_____

_____

_____

_____

_____

_____

_____

_____

Extended Response Question 2

What are some differences between polar bears and black bears?

_____

_____

_____

_____

_____

_____

_____

_____

_____

_____

Extended Response Question 3

Which bear do you prefer? Explain why.

_____

_____

_____

_____

_____

_____

_____

_____

_____

_____

Essay Sections

(Parents: Use the rubric at the end of this chapter to judge what your child's score would be.)

Extended Response Essay 1

Tell about a time you met someone new for the very first time. How did you feel beforehand? How did you feel when you finally met the person?

_____

_____

_____

_____

_____

_____

_____

_____

_____

_____

Extended Response Essay 2

Write a persuasive essay telling someone why he or she should read your favorite book.

_____

_____

_____

_____

_____

_____

_____

_____

_____

_____

Extended Response Essay 3

Write a detailed, descriptive story about your favorite day of the year. It can be a holiday, your birthday, the first day of summer vacation, etc. Be sure to give many good reasons why this is your favorite day.

_____

_____

_____

_____

_____

_____

_____

_____

_____

_____

Answers

Short Response Question 1

Some examples of answers could be:

- ▶ The ant took pity on the grasshopper and felt sorry for him, so he decided to help the grasshopper.
- ▶ The ant helped the grasshopper because it was the right thing to do.
- ▶ The ant was proud that the grasshopper finally took his advice and decided to reward the grasshopper.
- ▶ The ant was afraid that the grasshopper would die so he helped him.

Short Response Question 2

Some examples of answers could be:

- ▶ The grasshopper could make it up to the ant by gathering all the food the next summer and letting the ant play in the sunshine.
- ▶ The grasshopper could repay the ant by cleaning and doing all the repairs on the anthill all winter.

Short Response Question 3

An example of an answer could be:

- ▶ The ant found food by searching the meadow far and wide, from sunrise to sunset.

Extended Response Question 1

An example of a good answer could be:

When I was about six years old, I remember my mother telling me that I always had to wear a helmet when I rode my bicycle. I told her that it bothered me and was annoying and I didn't want to wear it. It also made my hair look funny when I took it off.

But my mom was adamant. She said, "Take my advice—always wear the helmet." So I did, but only when she was looking! When I would get around the corner I would take that bothersome helmet off and hang it on the handlebars.

One sunny day I went around the corner and took my helmet off as usual. But on that day, a strange dog came leaping over the neighbor's fence and started chasing me! He chased me right back to my house. I was so nervous I swerved and hit a rock, and I went sailing over the handlebars and landed on my head!

My mom came screaming out of the house. The dog ran away, but I got a huge cut on my forehead. I needed five stitches. I really learned the hard way that I should have taken my mother's advice and worn the helmet. Next time when she tells me something like that, I will be sure to listen.

Extended Response Question 2
An example of a good answer could be:

I think that the ant was very kind and caring, and this can be seen in his treatment of the grasshopper. The grasshopper fooled around all summer without regard to the future, and the ant worked very, very hard to prepare for the winter. He behaved nobly when he showed kindness to the grasshopper and gave him food when he was starving.

I would like to think I would be as noble as the ant if I had a friend who was starving, regardless of whether the friend listened to my good advice or not. I think that I would share my food if I were in the same situation.

The grasshopper, on the other hand, was very childish. He played and danced all summer and did not live up to his responsibilities. His actions almost cost him his life. I would hope that I would not be so foolish if I were in the same situation. I would do my job first and take care of my responsibilities before I would go and play.

Extended Response Question 3
If you chose the first option, your answer can be something like this:

I think that the moral of "The Ant and The Grasshopper" is not to put off what you should do today. This is exactly what the grasshopper did. He played and danced all summer long when he should have been gathering food.

Whenever the ant reminded him that he should be getting ready for winter right away, the grasshopper would always put it off. He would completely ignore the ant's good advice and continue to frolic in the sunshine.

When he finally realized that the ant was right, it was too late. He should not have put off his responsibilities; he should have taken care of them right away.

If you chose the second option, your answer can be something like this:

I think the moral of the story is, "Do your work before you play." This is what the ant was trying to teach the grasshopper.

The ant was working very hard all summer. He knew that there would be time to relax later, on a cold winter day when he had to stay in his ant hole. But he knew he had work to take care of first; namely, gathering food for the winter so he wouldn't starve.

The grasshopper didn't learn this until the very end of the summer. Then he realized the ant was right. Because he played first instead of doing his work, which was to gather food for the winter, he almost starved to death. I think that the grasshopper really learned this lesson, to do your work before you play.

Short Response Question 1

An example of an answer could be:

▶ Bats hunt using echolocation instead of eyesight. Echolocation is when a bat sends out a high-pitched sound, and the sound bounces back to tell the bat where its prey can be found.

Short Response Question 2

An example of an answer could be:

▶ Birds have bones that are hollow.

Short Response Question 3

An example of an answer could be:

▶ Bats sleep during the day because they are nocturnal. They usually sleep hanging upside down.

Short Response Question 4

An example of an answer could be:

▶ A mother bat nurses her baby bat. The baby bat drinks its mother's milk just like a real baby can.

Extended Response Question 1

An example of a good answer could be:

Bats and birds differ in many ways. Bats are mammals and give birth to live young. Birds hatch out of eggs. Mother bats nurse their young and mother birds chew food and put it into their babies' mouths. Bats hunt by using echolocation, where the bat sends out a high-pitched sound and it bounces back to them. This helps them locate things. Birds on the other hand, use their eyesight to hunt. Bats are covered with fur or hair, and birds have feathers.

Bats have teeth, but birds do not. Birds have beaks. Birds have hollow bones and bats do not. Bats have wings and hands, but birds only have wings. Lastly, bats are awake during the night. They are nocturnal. Birds sleep at night and are awake during the day.

Extended Response Question 2

An example of a good answer could be:

Bats and birds are both animals that can fly. They are both warm-blooded and they are also both vertebrates. They both like to eat bugs, small birds, fruit, and nectar. Some birds and some bats also migrate during the winter. This means they fly to warmer climates. Lastly, both birds and bats help with seed dispersal and insect control.

Extended Response Question 3
A sample of a good answer would be:

Even though I do not fly, I am more like a bat than a bird. Bats and people are both mammals. We have live young. Humans do not lay eggs like birds. And mothers can nurse their babies just like mother bats nurse their baby bats. And my mother never put chewed food into my mouth from hers!

I have hair but I do not have feathers. I also have hands, which bats have but birds do not. I have teeth, which bats have. Birds have a beak with no teeth. And I do not have hollow bones. Even though I do not sleep upside down during the day or use echolocation, I think I still am more similar to a bat than a bird.

PASSAGE THREE

Short Response Question 1
An example of an answer could be:

▶ Jellyfish are not really fish. Jellyfish are invertebrates, like sea anemones and coral.

Short Response Question 2
An example of an answer could be:

▶ Jellyfish move by pushing their bells in and out. They are also carried by the current and the wind.

Short Response Question 3
An example of an answer could be:

▶ The tentacles of a jellyfish contain stinging cells, which release venom to paralyze the jellyfish's prey.

Extended Response Question 1
An example of a good answer could be:

Jellyfish are made of two parts, the bell and the tentacles. Most of them are small, with short tentacles and bells that are about one to twenty inches across. Very few, however, have been found to have bells that reach as high as six feet across and tentacles that are over one hundred feet long.

Extended Response Question 2
An example of a good answer could be:

Many different creatures prey upon jellyfish, including birds, fish and turtles. Dogfish, cod, mackerel, and ocean sunfish are some fish that like to eat Jellyfish. Sea turtles also like to eat jellyfish. And sea birds and puffins eat jellyfish as well.

Extended Response Question 3
An example of a good answer could be:

To get food, the jellyfish raises and lowers its tentacles, and when the tentacles touch something, the jellyfish stings it. Some scientists used to think that jellyfish just drifted until their tentacles just happened to touch something. But now they know that at least a few species of jellyfish can follow the faint chemical trails laid down by zooplankton.

READ AND COMPARE TWO PASSAGES

Extended Response Question 1
An example of a good answer could be:

There are many similarities between black bears and polar bears. They are both large mammals. This means that they both give birth to live young, they do not lay eggs. They also both nurse their babies.

Both polar bears and black bears hibernate for many months during the winter. Mother polar bears and mother black bears both usually give birth to twins over the winter. And both kinds of bears can eat plants and animals, even though a polar bear prefers to eat meat.

Both polar bears and black bears are very large and weigh hundreds of pounds. They both can live up to 25 years in the wild as well.

Extended Response Question 2
An example of a good answer could be:

Even though polar bears and black bears are both bears, there are many differences between the two. Polar bears are much bigger than black bears. Polar bears can be up to ten feet long and weigh up to 1,700 pounds, whereas a black bear only goes up to six feet long and weighs an average of 125 to 600 pounds.

Polar bears are also much more fierce than black bears. Polar bears are the largest land carnivore, and they are great hunters, while black bears are relatively harmless. A polar bear mostly eats meat, like seals, and occasionally eats young walruses and beluga whales. They will also eat reindeer, rabbits, and birds. A black bear, on the other hand, prefers a wider variety of food, like plants, leaves, grasses, fruits, berries, nuts, roots, honey, carrion, insects, insect larvae, and other small mammals.

Another difference is that polar bears are usually white and are adapted for living in the artic, and black bears are usually black and live in the forests.

Extended Response Question 3
An example of a good answer could be:

I really like polar bears much more than black bears. Polar bears are fierce and powerful hunters. They are big and strong, much bigger and stronger than a black bear. They can even kill a whale, and knock out a seal in just one swipe!

I also like them because they are so smart. They know they have to blend in with the snow when they are stalking an animal, and they already know that their fur blends in. But they are also smart enough to know that they have to hide their noses, which they do! A polar bear will hide its nose by covering it with snow.

Polar bears are big, powerful and smart, and they are also great swimmers. They are interesting and incredible animals.

Rubrics

Rubrics vary from state to state, but in general they are very similar. Basically, in order to get a top score, your child has to respond to a question in an imaginative, logical, organized way. He or she has to use relevant support material, varied sentence structure, good vocabulary, and have few if any errors in punctuation, paragraphing, capitalization, grammar, and usage. Educators are well trained in using the rubrics that help them determine a score for your child. On the rubric that follows, you will see that each score is well defined. Teachers are also given certain "anchor" papers that your state educational department prepares as models. So, the grade your child receives should be very accurate. If you have trouble determining a correct score, you should see your child's teacher for some guidance. If you feel that your child's score is low, you might want to get some extra help. If it is high, that's great! Encourage your child to keep reading. Good literature and nonfiction are excellent models for everyone.

GENERIC RUBRIC FOR WRITING PROMPTS

CATEGORY	KNOWLEDGE AND UNDERSTANDING	ORGANIZATION	USE OF SUPPORT MATERIAL	SENTENCE STRUCTURE	VOCABULARY	GRAMMAR
Description	While writing a response, your child exhibits an understanding and interpretation of the task.	While writing a response, your child develops ideas with a coherent, logical, and orderly approach.	While writing a response, your child exhibits effective use of relevant and accurate examples to support ideas.	While writing a response, your child uses varied sentence structure.	While writing a response, your child uses effective language and challenging vocabulary.	While writing a response, your child uses conventional spelling, punctuation, paragraphing, capitalization, grammar, and usage.
4.0	Your child has a good understanding of the topic and writes about it in an imaginative and creative way.	Your child has organized and developed his/her ideas in a coherent and well-defined manner.	Your child purposely uses support material from the story that is relevant and appropriate.	Your child shows the ability to vary sentence structure.	Your child uses sophisticated vocabulary.	Your child makes few mechanical errors, if any.
3.0	Your child shows an understanding of the topic and writes about it in a logical, practical way.	Your child had an obvious plan to develop his/her idea that was satisfactory.	Your child has used some support material in an organized form.	Your child has used correct sentence structure, but there is little sentence variety.	Your child shows an average range of vocabulary.	Your child makes some mechanical errors, but they do not interfere with communication.
2.0	Your child tries to develop the topic but digresses and writes about other topics as well.	Your child shows little organization and development of content.	Your child does not use relevant support material for the narrative.	Your child shows some knowledge of sentence structure but also writes in fragments or run-on sentences.	Your child uses inaccurate, inexact, or vague language.	Your child makes many mechanical errors that interfere with communication.
1.0	Your child only addresses the topic minimally.	Your child shows no ability to organize or develop ideas.	Your child has not included or organized support material.	Your child does not have a sense of sentence structure.	Your child uses inexact or immature language.	Your child makes mechanical errors that make the paper impossible to understand.
0.0	A ZERO paper would be one that shows no relation to the topic, is illegible, incoherent, or blank.	A ZERO paper would be one that shows no relation to the topic, is illegible, incoherent, or blank.	A ZERO paper would be one that shows no relation to the topic, is illegible, incoherent, or blank.	A ZERO paper would be one that shows no relation to the topic, is illegible, incoherent, or blank.	A ZERO paper would be one that shows no relation to the topic, is illegible, incoherent, or blank.	A ZERO paper would be one that shows no relation to the topic, is illegible, incoherent, or blank.

Scores, Studies, Lists, and More

Interpreting Your Child's Score

WHEN YOU receive your child's scores in the mail, you may wonder what they mean and how you should decipher them. Understandably, interpreting test scores can be very confusing for parents unused to educational terms. These notes can guide the way for anyone puzzled by the new standardized test language.

Your child will receive a score of 1 to 4 on the test.

▶ A score of 1 or 2 is considered below standard.
▶ A score of 3 is proficient.
▶ A score of 4 is highly proficient.

The results of your child's test should be mailed to you within a few months of the actual test date.

Children who score a 1 or a 2 on the test are entitled to receive extra help from the school district. Parents of students who score a 1 or a 2 must be contacted, and in most states the school district is responsible for providing extra help for the child. That could include before or after school help, extra help during the school day, or even summer school. The state tests also help identify students who will need additional assistance meeting that particular state's standards. If your child does not do well on the test, the test alone should not be used to decide whether your child is promoted.

Points to Remember

Children actually prepare for standardized tests throughout grades K–3. It's never a good idea to "cram" for a test. The best way for parents to help is to reinforce learning by introducing some fun activities—that turn into lifelong learning habits—at home to help strengthen children's abilities in reading, writing, and listening.

Here are some ways to help:

▶ Have your child explain what he reads in a newspaper or a magazine article.
▶ Help your child keep a journal. Let him pick out his own special book to use.
▶ Leave messages around the house for your child to answer in writing.
▶ Play word games during car trips.
▶ Read aloud to your child. This helps you monitor progress in reading.
▶ Help your child get started on a writing assignment by asking questions.
▶ Carry a book to the doctor's office. Act as a role model for your child.
▶ Discuss literature with your child by asking:
  ◆ what the story is about
  ◆ for a description of the main character
  ◆ how the main character changed your child's ideas
  ◆ how the book was the same as or different from your child's life
  ◆ for a prediction about the ending before your child finishes the book
  ◆ what the sequel might be about

For more ideas, go to your child's teacher for help and advice; browse the Internet; join your local parent-teacher organization; and by all means, attend school events. Parents and teachers need to work together to make sure our children have everything they need to meet the new state standards.

HOME ACTIVITIES

Habits like these help your child at home:

▶ Limit television and video games.
▶ Encourage children to talk about what they are reading.
▶ Make sure your children finish their homework.
▶ Have discussions with your children about their studies.

▶ Remember that you can't be too involved with your children and what they are learning and doing. Make sure you stay on top of things. This may be easier said than done, but it is so important to ensure future success.

Fun (and Educational) Math Activities that Can Be Found in Everyday Life

Math is such a part of everyday life that sometimes we take no notice of just how often we use it. Doing math can sometimes be almost like a game, and we know that children love to play games. If we play math games with our children, they will be so busy having fun that they won't even realize they are learning.

LET'S START IN THE KITCHEN

Recipes
▶ The first thing that may come to your mind is the old recipe math. For good reason. It is an excellent way to incorporate math into everyday life, and it serves a useful purpose as well. Not only can you double and triple recipes, but you can halve them and quarter them as well. Your child will get to measure liquid and dry ingredients (good practice for science as well), and when the finished product comes out of the oven, he or she can help you divide it. After baking a pan of brownies, have your child divide the pan into 24 pieces. Point out that there are three different ways to cut them.

Coupons
▶ Have your child cut out some coupons you don't need, so he or she can play with them. Ask your child to add them up. Choose a type of food to have "double coupons"—for example, all cereal coupons are doubled today, so how does that change your total?
▶ You can also play store. Get some boxes and cans of food and attach Post-its on which to write prices. Then take turns being the customer and the cashier. The only catch here is that the cashier doesn't get to use an electronic cash register; he has to either use paper or do it in his head. You can make a game to see if you can get away with overcharging each other, and the customer has to be really sharp to catch a cashier who might have made a mistake. (Unfortunately, this is good practice for real life too!) And, if you want, you can pay with real money and figure out the correct change.

Cleaning
▶ If you have to clean the floor, you can have your child figure out how to dilute the concentrated cleaner.

Grocery Shopping

▶ If you get tired of playing the shopping game at home, you can take your child to the grocery store with you. She can either take along a calculator to figure out the exact amount of the groceries, or she can estimate the cost in her head. You can have a contest with estimating—who comes the closest without going over. You can also teach her how to figure out tax.

Games

▶ Rolling dice is always fun. One game you can play is to take turns rolling dice and adding them up. You can use two, three, or four dice. And to make it interesting, you can purchase dice that don't have six sides. They are very inexpensive, and your child may enjoy rolling a four-sided die or a twenty-sided die. And this game isn't only good for addition. You can say something like, "Take the number that appears on the twenty-sided die and subtract the number that appears on the six-sided die."

▶ You can also let your child be the banker when it comes to playing regular games such as Monopoly or Payday.

Balancing the Checkbook

▶ You can get a blank checkbook and give it to your child to use. You can start her off with a certain amount. Then—to make it like real life—give her some pretend bills to pay. She has to subtract the amount of the check, and then write out pretend checks. Children love this kind of thing, and you don't have to worry about being particularly artistic when it comes to making the checks for them.

Other Games

▶ Another game you can play is to have a contest adding two and three digit numbers. The catch is that your child gets to add them on paper but you have to add them in your head. The first one with the correct answer is the winner.

Grade Level Reading Lists

All teachers and administrators hope that your child will become a lifelong learner, and one of the best ways for this to happen is to encourage your child to read. The following list is an excellent choice of books—on many levels and in many genres—that you and your child can choose from. You should be able to find all of these books at your public library.

Picture Books

Ahlberg, Janet, Allan Alhberg, *The Baby's Catalogue*
Allard, Harry, James Marshall, *Miss Nelson is Missing!*
Barton, Byron, *Airport*
Brett, Jan, *The Mitten: An Ukranian Folktale*
Carle, Eric, *The Very Busy Spider*
DeGroat, *Alligator's Toothache*
Devlin, Wende, Harry Devlin, *Cranberry Thanksgiving*
Ehlert, Lois, *Feathers for Lunch*
Freeman, Don, illustrator, *Corduroy*
Hayes, Ann, Karmen Thompson (illustrator), *Meet the Orchestra*
Kellogg, Steven, *Johnny Appleseed*
Marshall, James, *George and Martha (Sandpiper Books)*
McCloskey, Robert, *Blueberries for Sal*
Munsch, Robert, Michael Martchenko (illustrator), *Thomas' Snowsuit (Munsch for Kids Series)*
Polacco, Patricia, *Babushka's Doll (Aladdin Picture Books)*
Siebert, Diane, Mike Wimmer (illustrator), *Train Song*
Steig, William, *Dr. DeSoto (A Sunburst Book)*
Tolen Brown, Marc, *Arthur's Tooth*
Waber, Bernard, *Ira Sleeps Over*
Wells, Rosemary, *Max's Chocolate Chicken*
Wiesner, David, *Hurricane*
Williams, Vera B., *A Chair for My Mother*
Williams, Sue, Julie Vivas (illustrator), *I Went Walking*

Caldecott Award Winning Picture Books

1995 Eve Bunting and David Diaz, *Smoky Night*
1994 Emily Arnold McCully, *Mirette on the High Wire*
1993 David Wiesner, *Tuesday*
1992 David Macaulay, *Black and White*
1991 Ed Young, *Lon Po Po*
1990 Karen Ackerman, *Song and Dance Man*
1989 Jane Yolen, *Owl Moon*
1988 Arthur Yorinks, *Hey, Al*
1987 Chris VanAllsburg, *The Polar Express*
1986 Margaret Hodges, *Saint George and the Dragon*
1985 Alice and Martin Provensen, *The Glorious Flight: Across the Channel with Louis Bleriot*
1984 Blaise Cendrars, *Shadow*

1983 Chris Van Allsburg, *Jumanji*
1982 Arnold Lobel, *Fables*

Beginning Reader Book List

These books have 44 words or less and are perfect for children who are just learning how to read.

Berenstain, Stan and Jan, *Bears on Wheels*
Cox, Mike, *Flowers*
Cohen, Caron Lee, *Three Yellow Dogs*

Early Start Readers:
A Happy Day
Jumping
The Tent

First-Start Reader:
Freddie the Frog
My Secret Hiding Place

Funny Farm Book:
Bag the Lamb
Hillert, Margaret, *The Yellow Boat*
Kim, Joy, *Rainbows and Frogs*
Ladybird, *Play With Us*
Le Seig, Theodore, *The Eye Book*
McKissak, Pat, *Who is Coming?*

Rookie Readers:
Bugs!
Fast Draw Freddie
Hi Clouds
Please, Wind?

Seuss, Dr.:
The Foot Book
Hop on Pop

Sunshine:
Ice Cream
Shopping
What's in This Egg
Willoughby, Alana, *My Dolly*

Kindergarten

Some kindergarteners may be able to read these books all alone, while others may need a parent or a teacher read to them.

Tumble Bumble by Felicia Bond
Kissing Hands by Audrey Penn
Owl Babies by Martin Waddell
My Very First Mother Goose edited by Iona Opie, illustrated by Rosemary Wells
Rainbow Fish and Rainbow Fish to the Rescue by Marcus Pfister
Will I Have a Friend? by Miriam Cohen
William's Doll by Charlotte Zolotow
Any of Eric Carle's books
Corduroy by Don Freeman
Farmer Duck by Martin Waddell
Rosie's Walk by Pat Hutchins
Chicken Soup With Rice: A Book of Months by Maurice Sendak
Ira Sleeps Over by Bernard Waber
Is Your Mama a Llama? by Deborah Guarino
Big Fat Hen by Keith Baker
Where's My Teddy? by Jez Alborough
Any *Carl* book by Alexandra Day
Runaway Bunny by Margaret Wise Brown
In the Rain With Baby Duck by Amy Hest
Leo the Late Bloomer by Robert Krauss
Any Dr. Seuss book
Any of Rosemary Wells' *Max* books
Go Away Big Green Monster by Ed Emberley
Oonga Boonga by Freida Wishinsky
How Joe the Bear and Sam the Mouse Got Together by Beatrice Schenk DeRegniers
Alphabet City by Stephen Johnson
First Snow by Kim Lewis
Lilly's Purple Plastic Purse by Kevin Henkes
Any of Norman Bridwell's *Clifford* books
Mooncake by Frank Asch
On Market Street by Arnold Lobel
When Daddy Took Us Camping by Julie Brillhart
Polar Bear, Polar Bear, What Do You Hear? by Bill Martin
Armadillo Rodeo by Jan Brett (or any of Jan Brett's books)
Have You Seen My Duckling? by Nancy Tafuri
Charlie the Caterpillar by Dom DeLuise
Any books by Ezra Jack Keats

Grade One Reading List

Aardema, Verna, *Borrequita and the Coyote*
Ackerman, Karen, *Song and Dance Man*
Adam, Barbara, *The Big, Big Box*
Andersen, Hans Christian, *The Ugly Duckling*
Anderson, C.W., *Billy and Blaze*
Anderson, Lonzo, *Two Hundred Rabbits*
Averill, Esther, *The Fire Cat*
Bailey, Carolyn, *The Little Rabbit Who Wanted Red Wings*
Baker, Betty, *Little Runner of the Longhouse*
Beim, Jerrold, *Andy and the School Bus*, *Two Is a Team*
Bemelmans, Ludwig, *Madeline*
Berenstain, Stan, *The Bears Vacation*
Bonsall, Crosby, *The Case of the Hungry Stranger*
Bridwell, Norman, *Clifford the Big Red Dog*
Bright, Robert, *Georgie*, *My Red Umbrella*
Brown, Marc, *Arthur Meets the President*
Brunhoff, Jean De, *The Story of Babar*
Burton, Virginia, *The Little House, Mike Mulligan and His Steam Shovel*
Cohen, Miriam, *Lost in the Museum*
Cole, Joanna, *The Missing Tooth*
Crews, Donald, *Big Mama's Truck*
De Paola, Tomie, *The Art Lesson*
De Regniers, Beatrice, *May I Bring A Friend?*
Dominska, Jania, *Turnip*
Duvoisin, Roger, *Petunia*
Eastman, P. D., *Are You My Mother?*
Ehlert, Lois, *Red Leaf, Yellow Leaf?*
Ehrlich, Fred, *Lunch Boxes*
Emberley, Barbara, *Drummer Hoff*
Ets, Marie, *Play With Me*
Farley, Walter, *Little Black, a Pony*
Fatio, Louise, *The Happy Lion*
Flack, Marjorie, *The Story About Ping*
Flournoy, Valerie, *The Patchwork Quilt*
Freeman, Don, *Corduroy*
Gag, Wanda, *Millions of Cats*
Giff, Patricia Reilly, *Happy Birthday Ronald Morgan*
Grimm, Jacob, *Shoemaker and the Elves*
Handforth, Thomas, *Mei Lei*
Hayword, Linda, *Hello House!*
Henkes, Kevin, *Chrysanthemum*

Heilbroner, Joan, *The Happy Birthday Present*
Heyward, DuBose, *Country Bunny and the Little Gold Shoes*
Hoban, Lillian, *Arthur's Loose Tooth*
Hoffman, Mary, *Amazing Grace*
Hoff, Syd, *Danny and the Dinosaur*
Holland, Marion, *A Big Ball of String*
Hopkins, Lee, *More Surprises*
Hutchins, Pat, *Rosie's Walk*
Isadora, Rachel, *At the Crossroads*
Johnson, Crockett, *Harold and the Purple Crayon*
Kahl, Virginia, *The Duchess Bakes a Cake*
Keats, Ezra, *A Letter to Amy*
Kellogg, Steven, *Prehistoric Pinkerton*
Kessler, Leonard, *The Big Mile Pace, Here Comes the Strikeout*
Konkle, Janet, *Schoolroom Bunny*
Krahn, Fernando, *The Mystery of the Giant Footsteps*
Kraus, Robert, *Whose Mouse Are You?*
Langstaff, John, *Frog Went a-Courtin!*
Le Sieg, Theodore, *Ten Apples Up On Top*
Lear, Edward, *The Owl and the Pussycat*
Lionni, Leo, *Inch by Inch, Swimmy*
Livingston, Myra, *Higgledy Piggledy*
Lobel, Anita, *The Pancake*
Lopshire, Robert, *Put Me in the Zoo!*
Maccarone, Grace, *The Sword in the Stone*
McCloskey, Robert, *Blueberries for Sal, Make Way for Ducklings*
Marshall, Edward, *Four on the Shore*
Minarik, Else, *Cat and Dog, Little Bear*
Ness, Evaline, *Exactly Alike, Josefina, February*
Nicholas, Paul, *Big Paul's School Bus*
Numeroff, Laura Joffe, *If You Give a Mouse a Muffin*
Potter, Beatrix, *The Tale of Peter Rabbit*
Ray, H.A., *Curious George*
Rice, Eve, *Benny Bakes a Cake, Goodnight, Goodnight!*
Rylant, Cynthia, *The Relatives Came*
Sawyer, Ruth, *Journey Cake, Ho!*
Schwartz, Amy, *Bea and Mrs. Jones*
Sendak, Maurice, *Where the Wild Things Are*
Seuss, Dr., *The Cat in the Hat, The Foot Book, Green Eggs and Ham,*
    Hop on Pop and collection
Smith, Ray, *The Long Slide*
Steig, William, *Amos and Boris, Sylvester and the Magic Pebble*
Tafuri, Nancy, *Have You Seen My Duckling!*

Thayer, Jane, *Where's Andy?*
Turkle, Brinton, *Thy Friend Obadiah*
Tworkov, Jack, *The Camel Who Took a Walk*
Udry, Janice, *The Moon Jumpers, A Tree is Nice, What Mary Jo Shared,*
    What Mary Jo Wanted
Van Allsburg, Chris, *The Polar Express*
Van Leeuwn, Jean, *More Tales of Amanda Pig*
Viorst, Judith, *Alexander and the Terrible, Horrible, No Good, Very Bad Day*
Watson, Jane, *Wonders of Nature*
Will and Nicholas, *Finders Keepers*
Winter, Paula, *The Bear and the Fly*
Wittman, Sally, *A Special Trade*
Wondriska, William, *Tomato Patch*
Worthington, Phoebe, *Teddy Bear Baker*
Yashima, Taro, *Crow Boy*
Yolon, Jane, *Owl Moon*
Young, Ed, *Lon Po Po*
Zaffo, George, *Harry and the Lady Next Door*
Ziefert, Harriet, *Goody New Shoes*
Zemach, Harve, *A Penny a Look, The Speckled Hen*
Zolotow, Charlotte, *Mr. Rabbit and the Lovely Present, William's Doll*

Grade 2

Aardema, Verna, *Why Mosquitoes Buzz in People's Ears*
Adler, David, *Cam Jansen and the Mystery of the Dinosaur Bones*
Allard, Harry, *Miss Nelson is Missing*
Andersen, Hans Christian, *The Princess and the Pea*
Anderson, C.W., *Billy and Blaze*
Aulaire, Ingrid, *Abraham Lincoln, George Washington*
Bailey, Carolyn, *Little Rabbit Who Wanted Wings*
Baker, Betty, *Little Runner of the Longhouse*
Bang, Molly, *The Paper Crane*
Barrett, Judith, *Cloudy With a Chance of Meatballs*
Beim, Jerrold, *Andy and the School Bus, Two is a Team*
Bemelmans, Ludwig, *Madeline*
Benchley, Nathaniel, *Sam the Minuteman*
Boegehold, Betty, *Pippa Mouse*
Bonsall, Crosby, *Case of the Hungry Stranger*
Brooks, Walter, *Henry's Dog Henry*
Brown, Marcia, *Shadow, Stone Soup*
Buller, Jon, *Baseball Cards Under the Sea*

Burton, Virginia, *The Little House, Mike Mulligan and His Steam Shovel*
Cameron, Ann, *The Stories Julian Tells*
Caudill, Rebecca, *Contrary Jenkins*
Chapman, Gaynor, *The Luck Child*
Christopher, Matt, *The Hit Away Kid*
Cole, Joanna, *The Magic School Bus Inside the Earth*
Credle, Ellis, *Down, Down the Mountain*
Daugherty, James, *Andy and the Lion*
Davis, Lavinia, *Roger and the Fox*
De Brunhoff, Jean, *Story of Babar*
De Paola, Tomie, *The Legend of the Paintbrush, Strega Nona, Tomie De Paola's
    Book of Poems*
DuBois, William Pene, *Bear Circus*
Duvoisin, Roger, *Petunia, Veronica*
Eastman, P.D., *Sam and the Firefly*
Fatio, Louise, *The Happy Lion*
Feelings, Muriel, *Jambo Meets Hello*
Fern, Eugene, *Peppito's Story*
Flack, Marjorie, *Story about Ping*
Gag, Wanda, *Millions of Cats*
Galdone, Paul, *Rumplestiltskin*
Giff, Patricia Reilly, *The Beast in Ms. Rooney's Room*
Goble, Paul, *The Girl Who Loved Wild Horses, Her Seven Brothers*
Grifaloni, Ann, *The Village of Round and Square House*
Grimm, Brothers, *Snow White and the Seven Dwarfs, Hansel and Gretel, Tom
    Thumb*
Guilfoile, Elizabeth, *Nobody Listens to Andrew*
Haley, Gail, *A Story, A Story*
Hall, Donald, *Ox Cart Man*
Handforth, Thomas, *Mei Lei*
Hastings, Selina, *Peter and the Wolf*
Heide, Florence, *The Shrinking of Treehorn*
Hest, Amy, *The Midnight Eaters*
Hodges, Margaret, *Saint George and the Dragon*
Holland, Marion, *A Big Ball of String*
Hooks, William, *Peach Boy*
Howe, James, *Harold and Chester in the Creepy Crawly Birthday*
Hurwitz, Johanna, *E, is for Elisa*
Jeffers, Susan, *Brother Eagle, Sister Sky*
Johnston, Troy, *Adventures of Mole and Troll*
Kahl, Virginia, *The Duchess Bakes a Cake*
Keats, Ezra Jack, *Dreams, A Letter to Amy*
Kellogg, Steven, *Johnny Appleseed, A Tall Tale*

Kimmel, Eric, *Hershel and the Hanukkah Goblins*
Leaf, Munro, *The Story of Ferdinand*
Lionni, Leo, *Inch by Inch*
Lipkind, Will, *Finders Keepers*
Lobel, Arnold, *Fables, Frog and Toad are Friends*
Marshall, James, *George and Martha*
McCloskey, Robert, *Blueberries for Sal, Make Way for Ducklings*
McDermott, Gerald, *Anasi the Spider, Arrow to the Sun*
Milhous, Katherine, *The Egg Tree*
Milton, Joyce, *Dinosaur Day*
Minarik, Else, *Little Bear*
Moore, Lilian, *I'll Meet You at the Cucumbers*
Morzallo, Jean, *Soccer Sam*
Mosel, Arlene, *The Funny Little Woman, Tikki Tikki Tembo*
Musgrove, Margaret, *Ashanti to Zulu*
Nobisso, Josephine, *Grandma's Scrapbook, Grandpa Loved*
Ness, Evaline, *Exactly Alike, Sam, Bangs, Moonshine*
O'Neill, Mary, *Hailstones and Halibut Bones*
Parish, Peggy, *Amelia Badelia*
Paterson, Katherine, *The Smallest Cow in the World*
Peet, William, *The Whingdingdilly*
Politi, Leo, *Song of the Swallows*
Potter, Beatrix, *Tale of Peter Rabbit*
Prelutsky, Jack, *The Random House Book of Poetry for Children*
Preston, Edna, *Toolittle*
Provenson, Alice, *The Glorious Flight*
Ransome, Arthur, *The Fool of the World and the Flying Ship*
Raskin, Ellen, *And it Rained, Who, Said Sue, Said Who?*
Renick, Marion, *Big Basketball Prize, Boy at Bat*
Rey, Hans A., *Curious George*
Ross, Pat, *M and M and the Halloween Monster, M and M and the Mummy Mess*
Ryan, Cheli, *Hillddilid's Night*
Rylant, Cynthia, *Henry and Mudge and the Bedroom Thumps, When I Was Young in the Mountains*
SanSouci, Robert, *The Talking Eggs*
Sawyer, Ruth, *Journey Cake, Ho!*
Seuss, Dr., *Green Eggs and Ham, Horton Hatches the Egg, Oh, the Places You'll Go! collection*
Sharmat, Marjorie, *Nate the Great*
Shub, Elizabeth, *The White Stallion*
Shute, Linda, *Clever Tom the Leprechaun*
Slobodkina, Esphyr, *Caps for Sale*
Snyder, Dianne, *Boy of the Three Year Nap*

Steig, William, *The Amazing Bone, Amos and Boris, Sylvester and the Magic Pebble*
Steptoe, John, *Mufara's Beautiful Daughters, An African Tale,*
    The Story of Jumping Mouse
Suhl, Yuri, *Simon Boom Gives a Wedding*
Trofimuk, Ann, *Babushka and the Pig*
Turnbull, Ann, *The Sand Horse*
Udry, Janice, *The Moon Jumpers*
Van Allsburg, Chris, *Jumanji*
Vioorst, Judith, *The Tenth Good Thing about Barney*
Waber, Bernard, *Lyle and the Birthday Party*
Ward, Lynd, *The Biggest Bear*
Whelan, Gloria, *Silver*
Williams, Barbara, *Albert's Toothache*
Wilson, Christopher, *Hobnob*
Wondriska, William, *Tomato Patch*
Wright, Mildred, *Sky Full of Dragons*
Yashima, Taro, *Crow Boy*
Yolen, Jane, *Commander Toad in Space, Greylings*
Zaffo, George, *Harry and the Lady Next Door*
Zelinsky, Paul, *Rumplestiltskin*
Zolotow, Charlotte, *Mr. Rabbit and the Lovely School*

Grade 3

Aesop, *Aesop's Fables*
Andersen, Hans C., *The Snow Queen, Thumbelina, The Wild Swans, and Collection*
Baylor, Byrd, *Hawk, I'm Your Brother*
Bishop, Claire, *Twenty and Ten*
Blume, Judy, *Freckle Juice, Fudge-a-Mania, Superfudge*
Bradbury, Bianca, *Two on an Island*
Brock, Emma, *Here Comes Kristie*
Brown, Jeff, *Flat Stanley*
Brown, Marcia, *Cinderella, Dick Whittington and His Cat*
Burchardt, Nellie, *Project Cat*
Bunting, Eve, *Summer Wheels*
Cameron, Ann, *Stories Julian Tells*
Carlson, Natalie, *Family under the Bridge*
Caudill, Rebecca, *Did You Carry the Flag Today, Charlie?, Happy Little Family*
Carroll, Ruth, *Beanie*
Christopher, Matt, *Baseball Flyhawk, Jack Rabbit Goalie*
Cleary, Beverly, *Ellen Tebbits, Henry Huggins, Ramona the Pest*
Clifton, Lucielle, *Lucky Stone*

Coatsworth, Elizabeth, *First Adventure*

Cone, Molly, *Mishmash*

Coombs, Patricia, *Dorrie and the Wizard's Spell*

Cooney, Barbara, *Chanticleer and the Fox*

Scieszka, Jon, *The Time Warp Trio: Knight of the Kitchen, The Time Warp Trio: The Not So Jolly Rancher*

Seligman, Dorothy, *Trouble with Horses*

Silverstein, Shel, *A Light in the Attic, Where the Sidewalk Ends*

Sleator, William, *Angry Moon*

Slobodkin, Louis, *Moon Blossom and the Golden Penny, The Space Ship under the Apple Tree*

Sobol, Donald, *Encyclopedia Brown, Boy Detective*

Sonneborn, Ruth, *Friday Night is Papa Night*

Stevenson, Robert Louis, *A Child's Garden of Verses*

Stockton, Frank, *The Griffon and the Minor Canon*

Thurber, James, *Many Moons*

Todd, Ruthven, *Space Cat*

Wagner, Jane, *J.T.*

Warner, Edythe, *Siamese Summer*

Weiss, Ellen, *The Adventures of Ratman*

White, E.B., *Charlotte's Web*

Wilber, Richard, *Loudmouse*

Wilder, Laura Ingalls, *Little House in the Big Woods*

Williams, Jay, The Practical Princess

Yolen, Jane, *The Sleeping Beauty*

Zemach, Harve, *Duffy and the Devil*

Manes, Stephen, *Be a Perfect Person in Just Three Days*

Marshall, James, *Rats on the Roof and Other Stories*

Mason, Marian, *A Pony Called Lighting*

Mathis, Sharon, *Hundred Penny Box*

McDermott, Gerald, *Anansi the Spider*

McKissack, Patricia, *Mirandy and Brother Wind*

Merrill, Jean, *Toothpaste Millionaire*

Miles, Miska, *Annie and the Old One, Hoagie's Rifle Gun*

Milhous, Katherine, *The Egg Tree, Song of the Swallows*

Monjo, F.N., *Poor Richard in France*

Moore, Lilian, *Everything Happens to Stuey*

Musgrove, Margaret, *Asshanti to Zulu*

Oleson, Claire, *For Pepita an Orange Tree*

Pinkwater, Daniel, *Blue Moose, Wempire*

Polisar, Barry, *Snakes: And the Boy Who Was Afraid of Them*

Prelutsky, Jack, *For Crying Out Loud*

Ransome, Arthur, *The Fool of the World and the Flying Ship*

Raskin, Ellen, *Spectacles*
Renick, Marion, *Big Basketball Prize, Pete's Home Run*
Schlein, Miriam, *Snake in the Car Pool*
Hodges, Margaret, *Saint George and the Dragon, The Wave*
Hogrogian, Nanny, *The Contest*
Honeycutt, Natalie, *The All New Jonah Twist*
Horvath, Betty, *Be Nice to Josephine, Not Enough Indians*
Howard, Ellen, *The Chickenhouse House*
Hunt, Mabel Leigh, *Benjie's Hat*
Hyman, Trina, *How Six Found Christmas*
Jackson, Caary, *Buzzy Plays Midget League Football, Little Leaguer's First Uniform*
Justus, May, *New Boy in School*
Kay, Helen, *A Summer to Share*
Keats, Ezra Jack, *John Henry, An American Legend*
Kingman, Lee, *The Best Christmas*
Kipling, Rudyard, *The Elephant's Child*
Kline, Suzy, *Herbie Jones*
Lattimore, Eleanor, *Little Pear, Peachblossom*
Lauber, Patricia, Champ, Gallant, Collie
Leichman, Seymour, *The Boy Who Could Sing Pictures*
Lexau, Joan, *Striped Ice Cream*
Lifton, Betty, *The Dwarf Pine Tree*
Lovelace, Maud, *Betsy Racy, The Valentine's Box*
Low, Alice, *Herbert's Treasure*
MacDonald, George, *The Light Princess*
MacLachlan, Patricia, *Sarah, Plain and Tall*
Dahl, Roald, *Fantastic Mr. Fox, James and the Giant Peach, The Minpins*
Dalgliesh, Alice, *Bears on Hemlock Mountain, The Courage of Sarah Noble*
De Angeli, Marguerite, *Bright April, Copper-Toed Boots*
Debois, William Pene, *The Alligator Case*
Edmonds, Walter, *The Matchlock Gun*
Embry, Margaret, *The Blue Nosed Witch*
Estes, Eleanor, *The Hundred Dresses*
Fall, Thomas, *Eddie No Name*
Felsen, Henry, *Cub Scout at Last*
Fife, Dale, *Who's in Charge of Lincoln?*
Flieschman, Sid, *McBroom and the Beanstalk*
Fritz, Jean, *And Then What Happened Paul Revere?*
Gannett, Ruth, *My Father's Dragon*
Giff, Patricia Reilly, *Purple Climbing Days*
Godden, Rumer, *Impunity Jane, Mouse House*
Greene, Constance, *Isabelle Shows Her Stuff*
Greenwald, Shelia, *Give Us a Great Big Smile Rosy Cole*

Grimm, Brothers, *Rapunzel, Snow White, Rose Red*

Haley, Gail, *A Story, A Story*

Haywood, Carolyn, *Betsy and Billy, Eddie and His Big Deals*

Heide, Florence, *Banana Twist, The Shrinking of Treehorn*

Hermschemeyer, Judtin, *Trudie and the Milch Cow*

Hicks, Clifford, *Peter Potts*

Grades 4–6

Alexander, Lloyd, *The Marvelous Misadventures of Sebastian, The Remarkable Journey of Prince Jen, The Philadelphia Adventure*

Armstrong, William, *Sounder*

Atwater, Richard and Florence, *Mr. Poppers Penguins*

Babbitt Natalie, *The Search for Delicious*

Blume, Judy, *Tales of a Fourth Grade Nothing, Fudge-a-Mania, Super Fudge, Blubber, Are You There God? It's Me, Margaret?, Then Again Maybe I Won't*, and collection

Burnett, Frances Hodgson, *The Secret Garden*

Byars, Betsy, *The Cybil War, Summer of the Swans, Coast to Coast, Beans on the Roof, A Blossom Promise, WANTED . . . Mud Blossom, The Two-Thousand Pound Goldfish*

Carlson, Natalie Savage, *The Family under the Bridge*

Cleary, Beverly, *Ramona, Ramona the Pest, Dear Mr. Henshaw, Henry and Ribsy, Henry Huggins, Ellen Tebbits*, and collection

Cohen, Barbara, *Thank You Jackie Robinson*

Collier, James Lincoln and Christopher, *My Brother Sam is Dead, The Clock, War Comes to Willie Freeman, Who is Carrie?*

Dahl, Ronald, *Danny the Champion of the World*

Houston, Jeanne Wakatsuda and James D., *Farewell to Manzanar*

Hurwitz, Johanna, *The Hot and Cold Summer and collection*

Ingalls, Laura, *The Collection*

Juster, Norton, *The Phantom Tollbooth*

LeGuin, Ursula, K., *Catwings*

Lewis, C. S., *The Chronicles of Narnia Series*

Lofting, Hugh, *The Story of Dr. Dolittle*

Lord, Betty Bao, *In the Year of the Boar and Jackie Robinson*

Lowry, Lois, *All About Sam, Anastasia Again, Number the Stars, Rabble Starkey*, and collection

Martin, Ann M., *Bummer Summer and collection*

Mendez, Phil, *The Black Snowman*

Montgomery, L.M., *Anne of Green Gables and the collection*

Noble, Trinka Hakes, *The Day Jimmy's Boa Ate the Wash*

O'Dell, Scott, *My Name is Not Angelica, The Black Pearl, Streams to the River, River to the Sea, Zia*

Paulson, Gary, *Woodsong, The Haymeadow* and Collection

Roberts, Willo Davis, *The Girl with the Silver Eyes*

Schwartz, David M., *If You Made a Million*

Silverstein, Shel, *Where the Sidewalk Ends*

Slepian, Jan, *The Alfred Summer*

Smith, Robert Kimmel, *Bobby Baseball, Mostly Michael, The Squeaky Wheel*

Snyder, Zilpha Keatley, *Fool's Gold, Libby on Wednesday, Song of the Gargoyle, The Diamond War*

Speare, Elizabeth George, *The Witch of Blackbird Pond*

Steinbeck, John, *The Red Pony*

Stevenson, Robert Louis, *Treasure Island*

Tate, Eleanora E., *Front Porch Stories at the One-Room School, Thank You Dr. Martin Luther King, Jr.!, The Secret of Gumbo Grove*

Taylor, Mildred, *Song of the Trees*

Taylor, Theodore, *The Cay*

Van Allsburg, Chris, *Jumanji*

White, E.B., *Charlotte's Web*

Woodruff, Elvira, *Awfully Short for the Fourth Grade, Back in Action, Dear Napoleon, I Know You're Dead, But . . .*

Wright, Betty Ren, *The Dollhouse Murders*

Easy Biographies for Grades K–3

Athletes

Adler, David A., *A Picture Book of Jesse Owens*

Esiason, Boomer, *A Boy Named Boomer*

Fuchs, Carol A., *Jackie Joyner-Kersee: Track and Field Star*

Harvey, Miles, *Hakeem Olajuwon: The Dream*

McCune, Dan, *Michael Jordan*

Rambeck, Richard, *Cal Ripken, Jr.*

Authors

Greene, Carol, *Laura Ingalls Wilder*

Greene, Carol, *Hans Christian Anderson*

Greene, Carol, *L. Frank Baum: Author of the Wonderful Wizard of Oz*

Martin, Patricia Stone, *Dr. Seuss, We Love You*

Meeks, Christopher, *Roald Dahl: Kids Love His Stories*

Rylant Cynthia, *Best Wishes*

Toby, Malene, *James M. Barrie: Author of Peter Pan*

Frontier

Adler, David, *A Picture Book of Davy Crockett*

Benjamin, Anne, *Young Pocahontas: Indian Princess*

Gleiter, Jan, *Annie Oakley*

Gleiter, Jan, *Kit Carson*

Gleiter, Jan, *Daniel Boone*

Greene, Carol, *Daniel Boone: Man of the Forests*

Historical Figures

Adler, David A., *A Picture Book of Patrick Henry*

Adler, David A., *A Picture Book of Christopher Columbus*

Adler, David A., *A Picture Book of Benjamin Franklin*

Adler, David A., *A Picture Book of Frederick Douglass*

Adler, David A., *A Picture Book of Paul Revere*

Adler, David A., *A Picture Book of Martin Luther King, Jr.*

Adler, David A., *A Picture Book of Robert E. Lee*

Behrens, June, *Barbara Bush: First Lady of Literacy*

Demarest, Chris, *Lindbergh*

Fritz, Jean, *And Then What Happened, Paul Revere?*

Fritz, Jean, *Will You Sign Here, John Hancock?*

Gleiter, Jan, *Sacagawea*

Greene, Carol, *Pocahontas: Daughter of a Chief*

Greene, Carol, *Sandra Day O'Connor: First Woman on the Supreme Court*

Hogrogian, Robert, *Molly Pitcher*

McLoone, Margo, *Frederick Douglass*

McKissack, Pat, *Booker T. Washington: Leader and Educator*

Nugent, Jean, *Prince Charles: England's Future King*

Schomp, Virginia, *Frederick Douglass: He Fought for Freedom*

Inventors

Adler, David A., *A Picture Book of Thomas Alva Edison*

Aliki, *A Weed is a Flower: The Life of George Washington Carver*

Fritz, Jean, *What's the Big Idea, Ben Franklin?*

Greene, Carol, *Benjamin Franklin: A Man with Many Jobs*

McLoone, Margo, *George Washington Carver*

Scarf, Maggi, *Meet Benjamin Franklin*

Musicians

Greene, Carol, *Ludwig van Beethoven*

Isadora, Rachel, *Young Mozart*

McKissack, Pat, *Louis Armstrong: Jazz Musician*

McKissack, Pat, *Marian Anderson: A Great Singer*

Rachlin, Ann, *Handel*

Rachlin, Ann, *Bach*
Rachlin, Ann, *Mozart*

Presidents

Adler, David A., *A Picture Book of George Washington*
Adler, David A., *A Picture Book of Abraham Lincoln*
Adler, David A., *A Picture Book of Thomas Jefferson*
Adler, David A., *A Picture Book of John F. Kennedy*
Behrens, June, *Ronald Reagan: An All-American*
Carrigan, Mellonee, *Jimmy Carter: Beyond the Presidency*
Cwiklik, Robert, *Bill Clinton: Our 42nd President*
Potts, Steve, *Franklin D. Roosevelt: A Photo-illustrated Biography*
Sabin, Louis, *Teddy Roosevelt: Rough Rider*

Women

Adler, David A., *A Picture Book of Anne Frank*
Adler, David A., *A Picture Book of Eleanor Roosevelt*
Adler, David A., *A Picture Book of Florence Nightingale*
Adler, David A., *A Picture Book of Helen Keller*
Adler, David A., *A Picture Book of Rosa Parks*
Adler, David A., *A Picture Book of Sojourner Truth*
Brown, Drollene P., *Sybill Rides for Independence*
Chadwick, Roxane, *Amelia Earhart: Aviation Pioneer*
Gleiter, Jan, *Annie Oakley*
McLoons, Margo, *Harriet Tubman*
McKissack, Pat, *Ida B. Wells-Barnett: A Voice Against Violence*
Quackenbush, Robert M., *Clear the Cow Pasture, I'm Coming in for a Landing: A Story of Amelia Eahrhart*
Behrens, June, *Barbara Bush: First Lady of Literacy*
Fuchs, Carol, *Jane Goodall: The Chimpanzee's Friend*
Gleiter, Jan, *Sacagawea*
Greene, Carol, *Pocahontas: Daughter of a Chief*
Greene, Carol, *Sandra Day O'Connor—First Woman on the Supreme Court*
Hogrogian, Robert , *Molly Pitcher*

State Departments of Education

Below are some sites that may help you find out more about the tests in your state.

ALABAMA TEACHER EDUCATION AND CERTIFICATION OFFICE

State Department of Education
P.O. Box 302101
Montgomery, AL 36130-2101
334-242-9935
www.alsde.edu

ALASKA DEPARTMENT OF EDUCATION

801 W. 10th Street, Suite 200
Juneau, AK 99801-1894
907-465-2831
www.educ.state.ak.us

ARIZONA DEPARTMENT OF EDUCATION

Arizona Department of Education
1535 West Jefferson Street
Phoenix, Arizona 85007
602-542-4361
800-352-4558
www.ade.state.az.us

ARIZONA DEPARTMENT OF EDUCATION – CERTIFICATION UNIT

Phoenix Office
P.O. Box 6490
Phoenix, 85005
602-542-4367
www.ade.state.az.us/certification

ARIZONA DEPARTMENT OF EDUCATION – CERTIFICATION UNIT

Tucson Office
400 W. Congress Street, #118
1535 West Jefferson
Tucson, AZ 85007
520-628-6326
www.ade.state.az.us/certification

ARKANSAS DEPARTMENT OF EDUCATION

General Education Division
Four State Capitol Mall, Room 304A
Little Rock, AR 72201-1071
501-682-4202
http://arkedu.state.ar.us

CALIFORNIA DEPARTMENT OF EDUCATION

721 Capitol Mall
Sacramento, California 95814
916-657-2451
www.cde.ca.gov

CALIFORNIA COMMISSION ON TEACHER CREDENTIALING

P.O. Box 944270
1812 9th Street
Sacramento, CA 94244-2700
916-445-7254
www.ctc.ca.gov

COLORADO DEPARTMENT OF EDUCATION

201 E. Colfax Avenue
Denver, CO 80203
303-866-6806
www.cde.state.co.us

CONNECTICUT STATE DEPARTMENT OF EDUCATION

165 Capitol Avenue
Hartford, CT 06145
860-566-5677
www.state.ct.us/sde

CONNECTICUT STATE DEPT. OF EDUCATION – PUBLIC INFORMATION OFFICE

P.O. Box 2219
Hartford CT 06145
860-713-6969
www.state.ct.us/sde/dtl/index.html

DELAWARE DEPARTMENT OF EDUCATION

John G. Townsend Building

P.O. Box 1402

Dover, DE 19903-1402

302-739-4601

www.doe.de.us

DISTRICT OF COLUMBIA TEACHER EDUCATION AND LICENSURE BRANCH

215 G Street NE, Suite 101A

Washington, DC 20002

202-724-4246

www.ed.gov

FLORIDA DEPARTMENT OF EDUCATION

Turlington Building

325 West Gaines Street

Tallahassee, FL 32399-0400

904-488-3217

www.firn.edu/doe

GEORGIA DEPARTMENT OF EDUCATION

205 Butler Street

Atlanta, GA 30334

404-656-2800

www.doe.k12.ga.us

HAWAII DEPARTMENT OF EDUCATION

P.O. Box 2360

Honolulu, HI 96304

808-586-3310

www.k12.hi.us

IDAHO DEPARTMENT OF EDUCATION

P.O. Box 8730

Boise, ID 83720-0027

208-332-6800

www.sde.state.id.us/Dept

ILLINOIS DEPARTMENT OF EDUCATION

100 W. Randolph, Suite 14-300

Chicago, IL 60601

312-814-2220

www.isbe.state.il.us

ILLINOIS BOARD OF EDUCATION

Division of Professional Preparation

100 N. First Street

Springfield, IL 62777-0001

217-782-2221

www.isbe.state.il.us

INDIANA DEPARTMENT OF EDUCATION

Professional Standards Board

State House, Room 229

Indianapolis, IN 46204-2798

317-232-9010

www.ideanet.doe.state.il.us

IOWA DEPARTMENT OF EDUCATION

Grimes State Office Building

De Moines, IA 50319-0416

515-231-5294

www.state.ia.us/educate

KANSAS DEPARTMENT OF EDUCATION

120 SE 10th Avenue

Topeka, KS 66612-1182

785-296-3201

www.ksbe.state.ks.us

KENTUCKY DEPARTMENT OF EDUCATION

Capital Plaza Tower

500 Metro Street

Frankfurt, KY 40601

502-564-4770

800-533-5372

www.kde.state.ky.us

LOUISIANA HIGHER EDUCATION AND TEACHING

P.O. Box 94064

Baton Rouge, LA 70804

504-342-3490

877-453-2721

www.doe.state.la.us/DOE/asps/home.asp

MAINE DIVISION OF CERTIFICATION AND PLACEMENT

Department of Education
23 State House Station
Augusta, ME 04333
207-287-5944
http://janus.state.me.us/education/homepage.htm

MARYLAND STATE DEPARTMENT OF EDUCATION

Certification Branch
200 W. Baltimore Street
Baltimore, MD 21201
410-767-0100
www.msde.state.md.us

MASSACHUSETTS DEPARTMENT OF EDUCATION

Office of Teacher Certification
350 Main Street
Malden, MA 02148
781-338-3000
www.doe.mass.us

MICHIGAN DEPARTMENT OF EDUCATION

608 W. Allegan Street
Hannah Building
Lansing, MI 43933
517-373-3354
www.mde.state.mi.us

MINNESOTA DEPARTMENT OF CHILDREN, FAMILIES, AND LEARNING

1500 Highway 36 West
Roseville, MN 55113
651-582-8200
www.educ.state.mn.us

MISSISSIPPI DEPARTMENT OF EDUCATION

Central High School
P.O. Box 771
359 North West Street
Jackson, MS 39205
601-359-3513
www.mde/k12.ms.us

MISSOURI DEPARTMENT OF ELEMENTARY AND SECONDARY EDUCATION

Division of Urban and Teacher Education—Teacher
  Certification
P.O. Box 480
Jefferson City, MO 65102
314-751-3486
www.dese.state.mo.us

MONTANA OFFICE OF PUBLIC EDUCATION

2500 Broadway
P.O. Box 200601
Helena, MT 59620
406-444-3150
www.metnet.state.mt.us

NEBRASKA DEPARTMENT OF EDUCATION

301 Centennial Mall South
P.O. Box 94987
Lincoln, NE 68509-4987
402-471-2295
www.edneb.org

NEVADA DEPARTMENT OF EDUCATION

700 East Fifth Street
Carson City, NV 89701-5096
702-486-6455
www.nsn.k12.nv.us/nvdoe

NEW HAMPSHIRE DEPARTMENT OF EDUCATION

Bureau of Credentialing
101 Pleasant Street
Concord, NH 03301-3860
603-271-3494
www.state.nh.us/doe

NEW JERSEY DEPARTMENT OF EDUCATION

Office of Licensing
P.O. Box
100 River View Plaza
Trenton, NJ 08625-0500
609-292-4041
www.state.nj.us/education

NEW MEXICO DEPARTMENT OF EDUCATION

Licensure Unit
Education Building
300 Don Gaspar
Santa Fe, NM 87501-2786
505-827-6587
http://sde.state.nm.us

NEW YORK STATE EDUCATION DEPARTMENT

Education Building
89 Washington Avenue
Albany, NY 12234
518-474-3852
www.nysed.gov

NORTH CAROLINA STATE DEPARTMENT OF PUBLIC INSTRUCTION

301 North Wilmington Street
Raleigh, NC 27601-2825
919-715-1246
www.dpi.state.nc.us

NORTH DAKOTA EDUCATION STANDARDS AND PRACTICES BOARD

600 E. Boulevard Avenue
Bismark, ND 58505-0440
701-328-2260
www.dpi.state.nd.us

OHIO DEPARTMENT OF EDUCATION

Teacher Education and Certification and Professional
   Development
65 Front Street South
Columbus, OH 43215-4183
877-644-6338
www.ode.state.or.us

OKLAHOMA STATE DEPARTMENT OF EDUCATION

Hodge Education Building
2500 N. Lincoln Boulevard
Oklahoma City, OK 73105-4599
405-521-3301
http://sde.state.ok.us

OREGON DEPARTMENT OF EDUCATION

Teacher Standards and Practices
255 Capitol Street NE
Salem, OR 97310-0203
503-378-3569
www.ode.state.or.us

PENNSYLVANIA DEPARTMENT OF EDUCATION

Bureau of Teacher Preparation and Certification
333 Market Street
Harrisburg, PA 17126-0333
717-787-3356
www.pde.psu.edu

RHODE ISLAND EDUCATIONAL DEPARTMENT

255 Westminster Street
Providence, RI 02903
401-222-4600
www.ridoe.net

SOUTH CAROLINA DEPARTMENT OF EDUCATION

1429 Senate Street
Columbia, S.C. 29201
803-734-8500
www.state.sc.us/sde

SOUTH DAKOTA DEPARTMENT OF EDUCATION

Kneip Building, 3rd Floor
700 Governors Drive
Pierre, SD 57501-2291
605-773-3134
www.state.sd.us/deca

TENNESSEE STATE DEPARTMENT OF EDUCATION

Andrew Johnson tower, 6th Floor
710 James Robertson Parkway
Nashville, TN 37234-0375
617-741-2731
www.state.tn.us/education

TEXAS EDUCATION AGENCY
William B. Travis Building
1701 N. Congress Avenue
Austin, TX 78701-1494
512-463-9734
www.tea.state.tx.us

UTAH STATE OFFICE OF EDUCATION
250 East 500 South
Salt Lake City, UT 84111
801-538-7517
www.state.ut.us/education.html

VERMONT DEPARTMENT OF EDUCATION
120 State Street
Montpelier, VT 05620-2501
802-828-3147
www.cit.state.vt.us/educ

VIRGINIA DEPARTMENT OF EDUCATION
101 N 14th Street
Richmond, VA 23218
804-225-2020
800-292-3820
www.pen.k12.va.us

WASHINGTON DEPARTMENT OF EDUCATION
P.O. Box 47200
Olympia, WA 98504-7200
360-586-4699
www.k12.wa.us

WEST VIRGINIA DEPARTMENT OF EDUCATION
1900 Kanawha Boulevard East
Charleston, WV 25305
304-558-2861
http://wvde.state.wv.us

WISCONSIN DEPARTMENT OF PUBLIC INSTRUCTION
125 S. Webster Street
Madison, WI 53702
800-441-4563
www.dpi.state.wi.us

WYOMING DEPARTMENT OF EDUCATION
2300 Capitol Avenue
Hathaway Building, 2nd Floor
Cheyenne, WY 82002-0050
307-777-7675
www.k12.wy.us

Give Yourself The LearningExpress Advantage

The Skill Builders Series is the solution for any job applicant needing to demonstrate basic language, math, or critical thinking competency---Likewise, high school students, college students or working adults who need to better their English and math skills to meet the demands of today's classroom or workplace will find the help they need in these easy-to-follow practice books.

Each Skill Builders volume offers:

- A complete 20-step program for mastering specific skills
- Quick and easy lessons that require a minimal time commitment—each lesson can be completed in just 20 minutes
- Supreme flexibility—users can take the whole course or customize their own individual study plan to meet specific goals or requirements